The Orderly Conversation

Praise for *The Orderly Conversation*®

"Where was this book when I was starting out?!? *The Orderly Conversation* provides a refreshing approach to speaking for the business professional—one that provides a pathway to tap our individual strengths and bring our authentic selves to every presentation. This could change the way people do business!"

Pamela Meyer, Ph.D.
Author, *From Workplace to Playspace: Innovating, Learning and Changing for Dynamic Engagement*

"*The Orderly Conversation* recognizes that the best presentations, like the best conversations, are dialogues rather than monologues that often take unexpected paths but produce invaluable insights. This book offers a way to stay true to your presentation's plan while still capitalizing on what's happening in the moment. By doing so it helps redefine the modern business presentation."

Dave Zielinski
Editor, PresentationXpert newsletter, www.presentationxpert.com

"As an instructional designer who specializes in developing communication skills, I have certainly had to scan many of the old fashioned 'do this, don't do this' self-help guides for presenters. *The Orderly Conversation* is miles beyond. This text explores what is really happening between a presenter and an audience. I can't say enough how much more powerful this book is than any other one I've seen on the subject. In a world of generic blends, these two guys are Single Malt Scotch."

Matt Elwell, CPLP
President and CEO, ComedySportz of Chicago, Inc.

"I sometimes wonder if there's any hope for professional communication in this modern era of presentation software, where we hide behind rigid outlines of bullets rather than truly converse with real people. It's exciting to finally see a work that challenges this persistent insanity. Dale and Greg's book resonates with a deep need I'm noticing among presenters today, a desperate desire to stop 'performing' and be real with audiences instead. Spread the word, gentlemen. If I had my way, your text would be required reading in every business school in the land."

Robert Lane
Director, Aspire Communications

"For many of us, facilitation skills come naturally. Or so we think. In truth, it's a slippery slope between excellent business presentations and immoral edutainment and trickery. With success comes laziness, and a tendency to throw content at our audience. Revive your most important business tool—the effective presentation—through this very actionable nuts and bolts book. I guarantee, when you open this book you'll find out you can still improve. *The Orderly Conversation* is an excellent way to do it."

Lou Russell
Queen, Russell Martin & Associates

"I believe this book is useful to business people at every level. The idea that a presentation is a conversation is unique and valuable. I'm excited to use what I've learned in my next presentation, and I'm buying several copies for my colleagues. Dale and Greg...Thank you!"

Nick Rosa
Managing Director, Sandbox Industries

"*The Orderly Conversation* is a peek into the personal experiences of several business professionals who, like me, struggled with communicating in a professional, yet compelling way. I really got to know these characters (and we became friends) on our journey to learn and apply some very simple and effective conversation techniques. You will use what you learn in *The Orderly Conversation* in the office, at home, and really anywhere the stakes are high and you need to get business done."

Antonia Fico
Director, Performance Solutions, US Cellular

"As a teacher of public speaking 101, I am quite familiar with the 'rules' for speaking that students learn in college. I have been trying to help students adapt these rules to their own styles and strengths for many years–and I really could have used the concepts in this book! In *The Orderly Conversation*, Dale Ludwig and Greg Owen-Boger are building the bridge so many have been looking for: the one between college speaking 101 and the real world. This book would be perfect as a text for Business Communication classes or as a supplement to the traditional 101 text. The book's emphasis on 'engagement' moves presenters away from the recitation of pre-packaged content, and points them toward a dynamic conversation that will empower both presenter and listener."

Kay Holley
Teacher of performance and communication for 36 years,
University of Illinois at Urbana-Champaign

"Forget what you've been taught about speech-making in a business setting. This book is about what really makes deals happen—the conversations between you, and your boss or your customers. *The Orderly Conversation* will turn your presentations into focused conversations that will have your audience engaged and supportive of your project, sale or proposal. Every consultant and manager will glean practical, immediately usable ideas from this book. A definite BUY review."

Drew S. Mendoza
Managing Principal, The Family Business Consulting Group, Inc.

"Challenging the traditional concept of business presentation as performance, the authors share practical techniques for engaging your audience in productive conversations. Free from tedious checklists and confining rules, their methods help you focus on what matters in business: results, and the connections that make them possible."

Mike Nalley
Computer Systems Analyst, City of Cincinnati, Ohio

"The ideas contained in *The Orderly Conversation* are unique in their approach and effective in their results. While most books on the subject stress how to look good speaking at people, *The Orderly Conversation* shows how to truly connect with people, so you can stop performing and start engaging. As a professional trainer for the past 15 years, I've spent thousands of hours honing my craft, and I wish I'd had this book earlier in my career as it would have saved me a lot of time and bad advice. If you present your ideas to others (and who doesn't?), then you need to read this book. It will make you a better communicator."

Blaine Rada
"America's Greatest Thinker," The Great American Think-Off

The Orderly Conversation

Business Presentations Redefined

Dale Ludwig
Greg Owen-Boger

Published by
Granville Circle Press
2811 University Ave. SE #14445 Minneapolis, MN 55414
info@granvillecirclepress.com

Printed in the United States of America and
distributed by Itasca Books www.itascabooks.com
1-800-901-3480

Quantity sales. Special discounts are available on quantity purchases. For details, contact the publisher at sales@granvillecirclepress.com.

Orders for textbook and course adoption. Contact the distributor at orders@itascabooks.com.

This Granville Circle Press book is printed on paper that contains 30% post-consumer fiber with FSC certification, manufactured using biogas energy. Printers are powered by energy harnessed on the wind farms of southwestern Minnesota.

ISBN: 978-0-9838703-2-6

Library of Congress Cataloging-in-Publication Data
Ludwig, Dale.
The orderly conversation : business presentations redefined / Dale Ludwig and Greg Owen-Boger.
pages cm
Includes bibliographical references and index.
ISBN: 978-0-9838703-2-6
1. Business presentations. 2. Public speaking. 3. Business communication.
4. Microsoft PowerPoint (Computer file) I. Owen-Boger, Greg. II. Title.
HF5718.22 .L831 2014
658.4`52—dc23

2014936280

Cover, interior design and illustrations: Brad Norr, www.bradnorrdesign.com
Indexer: Dianna Haught
Editor: Barbara Egel

Photos, page viii— David Rigg

Dedication

This book is dedicated to all the business presenters we have worked with since Turpin Communication's founding in 1992. During the time they spent with us, each of these people opened up about the work they do and the challenges they face. They tried new things. They shared their feelings, their fears and their breakthroughs. In doing so, they taught us a lot. Without them, this book would not exist.

About the Authors

Dale Ludwig and Greg Owen-Boger have been delivering presentation and facilitation skills training for a total of 41 years—that's 22 years for Dale and 19 for Greg. We're often asked if we deliver other types of training. Technically, the answer to that question is no. In the world of corporate learning and development, we work in a relatively narrow space.

Practically, though, our focus is as broad as the businesses and business people we work with. Working in this field for as long as we have, we've learned a lot about what it takes for business presenters to succeed and how we can help them achieve that success. Our passion for this work is reflected in our writing, speaking, training, and consulting.

Dale Ludwig has a Ph.D. in Communication and, prior to Turpin, taught at the University of Illinois at Urbana-Champaign. He founded Turpin Communication in 1992. Since then he has worked to keep Turpin focused on providing the best presentation and facilitation skills training available. In addition to his work in live, instructor-led workshops, Dale also appears in Turpin's eLearning courses.

Greg Owen-Boger has been with Turpin Communication since 1995, first as a cameraman, then instructor, and now vice president. Schooled in management and the performing arts, Greg brings a diverse set of skills and experience to the organization. He is a frequent blogger, and his work has appeared in *Master Presenter: Lessons from the World's Experts on Becoming a More Influential Speaker.*

We have decided to keep our voices separate throughout the text. Dale's voice is in a serif font (like this). Greg's is in sans serif (like this).

Contents

Introduction
Getting Business Done

The ideas in this book stem from the notion that when we talk about doing business, we're talking about an ongoing conversation. It is a conversation that takes place between organizations, between those who buy and those who sell, between manufacturers and distributors, between service providers and clients. It is also a conversation within organizations, between front-line managers and the people reporting to them, between marketing and sales, between the CEO and the board.

The business presentations you deliver are part of these larger conversations. They exist for one reason: to keep business moving forward. If they did not do that, there would be no need for them. For a business presenter, the stakes are high and the conversations need to go well.

As any book for business presenters should, *The Orderly Conversation®* will address PowerPoint slides, the nervousness you might face, delivery skills, organizational strategies, and recommendations for managing questions. But we will address these things in a new way, by helping you

- sharpen the distinction between the presentations you deliver now and the speeches you were taught to deliver in school. This will enable you to focus on the right goals and judge your success accordingly.

- challenge the assumption that practice either makes perfect or reduces nervousness. We will show you why perfection is an impossible goal and how nervousness can be managed in the moment it strikes.
- understand why your individual response to the challenges of presenting matters and how it can be managed.
- dig deeper into a process that for too long has been glossed over with tips and tricks. This information will help you understand not only what you need to do to improve, but why you need to do it.

Throughout this book, our goal is to help you, as the unique individual you are, get business done.

Contents

Chapter 1
Why You Need This Book

In this chapter . . .
- **Why *This* Book?**
- **The Evolution**
- **How We're Going to Proceed**

Dale:

This book is for business presenters, the people who deliver everyday, getting-business-done presentations. These presentations are used to close a sale, explain financial information, deliver project updates, or train internal audiences. Their topics and goals are as varied as the organizations in which they exist.

If you're a business presenter, you know that your presentations wouldn't mean very much to anyone outside the business, or sometimes even the business unit, where they are delivered. They are not formal speeches with a message intended to ripple out to a large, diverse audience. They are the opposite of that. Their purpose is to pull people together at a specific point in time to reach understanding, gain approval, or take whatever step needs to be taken. Business audiences crave simplicity and efficiency. When presentations are over, people want to go back to their desks feeling something was accomplished and their time was well spent.

By saying this, we don't mean to downplay the significance of business presentations nor place them on the lowest rung of the public speaking ladder. On the contrary, we want to recognize the very practical role of business presentations in your work and to assert that they are one of the most complex communication processes you need to master.

Many business presenters assume the challenge they face lies in the routine or mundane nature of the content they present. "This is the monthly financial report . . . not much to get excited about," they might say to us. However, their challenge has little to do with *what* they present. It has to do with the realities of the business environment. You've probably faced some of these situations:

- The meeting is running long, forcing you to make last-minute adjustments to the length of your presentation.
- It is clear from their behavior (texting, e-mailing, looking glum) that some audience members have little desire to listen to what you have to say.
- Some people at the meeting obviously have an agenda of their own.
- It seems the decision maker has already decided.
- You don't know your audience that well, which makes you nervous and unsure.
- You *do* know your audience well, which makes it easy for you to get a little lazy with preparation.

All of this can leave you standing at the front of the room feeling uncomfortable and wondering how to proceed. You might worry that you've underprepared. You might struggle to communicate content you know very well. You might deliver information so quickly your point isn't understood. You might get stuck on a single question and run out of time. In the end, you leave the presentation feeling frustrated with your audience or yourself.

This book will help you work through these problems. We can't change the people you work with or the business you work in, but we can make your presentations better and the work you do when preparing and delivering them easier. Our goal is simple. We want to make your business-presenter responsibilities no more challenging than any other part of your job.

Why This Book?

This book is unique for a couple of important reasons. First, it focuses on the type of presentations you actually deliver. Other resources available to you—books, blogs, academic courses, and the corporate training they have inspired—do not. They focus on speechmaking. Your presentations require a fundamentally different approach.

Therefore, much of what you have been taught about presenting has to be replaced. This includes, for example, the notion that a perfect presentation is possible, that practice will guarantee success, that graphic images on slides are always better than words, and that there are rules about where to stand and how to gesture. We'll talk about how these assumptions hamper your success.

We know how disconcerting it can be when you're asked to throw out what you assume is tried-and-true wisdom. However, if a particular way of thinking or a specific technique doesn't serve your needs, it has to go. We'll help you understand why and provide better alternatives.

Second, we respect your individuality. We know your strengths and weaknesses as a presenter are unique, and you will not improve in exactly the same way as anyone else. You will need to adapt the recommendations we offer here to fit you and your needs. We'll help you with that whenever we can.

The Evolution

The ideas in this book grew out of the work we do as presentation skills trainers and coaches. Most of the training we deliver takes place in small-group workshops. A standard class has eight participants. During the workshop, each of these eight people prepares and practices a real-life business presentation. It doesn't matter what that presentation is about or how large or small its audience might be. We ask only that the presentation be a current, active part of the person's work. Our workshops also include one-on-one coaching using video. Presenters are recorded on video as they work in front of the group, and then each person reviews the video privately with his or her coach. This process builds self-awareness and objectivity. It also helps presenters see what they already do well.

With these two aspects of our work—focusing on real-life content and using video—we are able to guide presenters through the complexity of business interactions and the nuances of their individual improvement. In doing this, we have learned not only how presenters struggle, but why. In response to what we've learned, our methodology has evolved. Over the years, small adjustments have added up to larger ones. Eventually, the larger ones came together to form something fundamentally new. This book is a reflection of that new thinking. In it we offer you a better way—a revolutionary way—for you to think about, prepare, and deliver your presentations.

Some portions, like this one, are written by me, Dale. Others, written by Greg, will track the progress of our workshop participants.

How We're Going to Proceed

The next two chapters are about why and how we're redefining business presentations. Following that, we will look at how that redefinition plays out at every stage of the process. We'll keep things as practical and focused as possible.

To do that, we have decided to keep our voices separate. Some portions, like this one, are written by me, Dale. The portions written by Greg will track the progress of eight imaginary people as they participate in one of our two-day presentation skills workshops. He will focus on how the ideas we're presenting are put into practice. As you read, keep in mind that although our eight presenters are fictional, their issues and concerns are very real and typical.

Here's a brief introduction:

Terry is the new Director of IT at his company and needs to find ways to be concise, especially when speaking to executives.

Dorothy is in market research and presents to a wiggly group of internal salespeople.

Michael sells energy bars and delivers seated presentations to distracted buyers.

Jennifer suffers from severe nervousness, and her new role requires monthly presentations.

James founded his business 30 years ago and is just now hearing that his presentations are disorganized.

Sophia has been training internal groups for years and doesn't understand why her manager sent her to this class.

Luis is a young entrepreneur who needs guidance on his next pitch to venture capitalists.

Elaine works for a real estate development company and presents sometimes controversial plans at town hall meetings.

By watching each of these presenters as he or she responds to the training and coaching received in the workshop, you're likely to recognize yourself in one or more of them. As they find ways to improve, you will too.

Contents

Chapter 2
Why We're Redefining

In this chapter . . .

- **A Speech Is a Type of Performance**
- **A Presentation Is a Type of Conversation**

Redefining the business presentation process began for us with a subtle shift in thinking. Here's how that happened:

In all of our workshops, a certain amount of unlearning has always taken place. Presenters come to us with specific ideas about what presentations are and how they should be managed. Some participants have been presenting for years. Some are new to it. Even if they have never delivered a business presentation, though, they have taken a public speaking class in school.

Some of the ideas presenters bring to the workshop are good, and we do our best to reinforce them. Some are not so good, and presenters struggle to apply them. Our job is to help presenters sift through what they know and what they've been told, separating the good from the bad, the generic from the useful. Here are some examples of what we mean.

- All presenters know they need to be well prepared, but most are unsure about what *well prepared* means for them. This uncertainty can lead to wasting time and not reaching the desired result.

- Presenters assume that the more they practice a presentation, the better it will be, so they often set themselves up for disappointment.
- Nervous presenters are confused and frustrated. The strategies they apply to control their anxiety fail them.
- Presenters assume there are hard-and-fast rules for effective delivery, even though following the rules doesn't feel right.
- For many presenters, the rules prescribed for visual aids are unrealistic. We hear this comment a lot: "I know I shouldn't have more than six bullet points on this slide, but I need eight to make my point."
- Some presenters try to change who they are. They might try to imitate other presenters and speechmakers. They might try to stop "talking with their hands," because someone told them they should. As a result, they wind up fighting against their natural strengths.
- Presenters have been taught to control the interaction that takes place during their presentations. In doing so, they might discourage a conversation that needs to happen.

Over time, we realized that everything we were helping presenters unlearn came from the world of speechmaking. Although presenters knew they were not delivering formal speeches, the assumptions they made and the strategies they used didn't reflect that. They were simply working with the wrong tools, like using the handle of a screwdriver to pound a nail into the wall. If you worked at it long enough, you might be able to do it, but why bother when there's a hammer in the toolbox?

At some point, probably when debriefing after a workshop, one of us said, "We should just stop calling these things *presentations* altogether. Everyone gets hung up on that word. Wouldn't it be easier to just call them *conversations*? That's really what they are."

So that's what we did. We brought the idea that business presentations are a type of conversation, not a type of speech, into our workshops. As we followed that line of thinking, we realized we were heading toward a major overhaul. From preparation and delivery, through managing interaction, to how you judge your success when the presentation is over—all of these things are affected when you begin with the assumption that what you're dealing with is a conversation.

"We should just stop calling these things *presentations* altogether. Everyone gets hung up on that word. Wouldn't it be easier to just call them *conversations*? That's really what they are."

The fundamental distinction is that a speech is a type of performance and a presentation is a type of conversation.

A Speech Is a Type of Performance

When you observe a performance of any kind—let's use stage actors as an example—everything you see and hear is planned, rehearsed, and controlled. During the performance, the world of the actor is kept separate from the world of the audience. Theater people call this separation "the fourth wall." From their seats in the theater, on their side of the wall, audiences observe. They never forget that the performer is performing, no matter how convincing the performance might be. Individuals in the audience can be moved by the final scene in *Romeo and Juliet*, for example, without worrying about whether the actor playing Juliet actually stabbed herself.

On the other side of the wall, up on the stage, actors are aware of their audience, and this awareness sharpens their performance. What it doesn't do is change the shape or direction of the performance itself.

A similar wall is in place when you watch a speech. Even though speechmakers address the audience directly, audience members know the speech has been scripted and rehearsed. Speechmakers succeed when the audience is attentive and feels good about the message and the speechmaker. Speechmakers are admired for their command of the stage, the power of their message, their polish and control—the very things we admire in actors.

In the business environment, leaders use speeches to set a new course for the organization or celebrate success. Like all speeches, they have big goals for a broad audience. If a speech fails to meet its goals with people in the audience, it's not a good thing, but at least the speech is over. Speechmakers don't return to the same group and deliver the speech again and again until it succeeds.

A Presentation Is a Type of Conversation

Presentations, on the other hand, are an exchange between a presenter and an audience. There is no fourth wall. Presenter and audience are fully engaged in the here and now of the conversation. This connection is present no matter how large the group might be or how much they interact with the presenter. Presenters cannot succeed—or succeed as fully as possible—unless this connection is made.

What this means is that the success of a presentation is measured in two ways. One level of success has to do with whether you reach your intended outcome. Let's say you're delivering a presentation to your team. Your job is to convince them that the project you're working on should go forward. To do that, you need to give them the evidence they need to make that decision.

Because you're asking your audience to do something—to listen, think, and give you the go-ahead—you also have a second goal. You need to make the work you're asking your team to do as easy as possible. This requires keeping the conversation fruitful and efficient. When presenters miss this goal—because they're distractingly uncomfortable, verbose, or unclear—it often means the work that needs to be done that day doesn't get done. Your project isn't approved, the sale isn't closed, the budget isn't agreed to, or the new process isn't learned. This leads to frustration and delay. In a lot of situations, that means coming back and trying again. Next time, though, you'll be carrying the baggage of the previous presentation with you.

The first step toward reaching your goals as a business presenter, then, is to be fully aware of the unique nature of this type of conversation. We'll focus on that step in the next chapter.

Contents

Chapter 3
Welcome to *The Orderly Conversation*

In this chapter . . .

- **Staying Buttoned Up while Keeping the Conversation Flowing**
- **So What Does This Mean for You?**

We chose the phrase "orderly conversation" to describe business presentations, because it focuses on the essential characteristics of the process. It's also a bit of an oxymoron, and we liked that quality about it, too. As you know, a typical conversation is not very orderly. It wanders off in more than one direction, building on itself along the way. It's free-flowing. It may return to the original topic, or it may not. Conversations thrive on the give-and-take among the people involved.

Your business presentations do the same thing, but the give-and-take happens in an orderly fashion, within a framework you have prepared in advance. A successful presentation, then, needs to be both buttoned up (orderly) and free-flowing (a conversation). The tension between the two, the fact that both things are happening at once, defines the process.

A successful presentation needs to be both buttoned up (orderly) and free-flowing (a conversation). The tension between the two, the fact that both things are happening at once, defines the process.

Staying Buttoned Up while Keeping the Conversation Flowing

The tension between order and conversation is best understood using three variables.

1. **Method of reception.** Does your audience read or listen?
2. **Level of spontaneity.** How much time separates preparation and delivery?
3. **Degree of participation.** How interactive is the process?

Let's compare writing a report for your boss and having a spontaneous conversation in the break room with her about the report. Let's say the topic is how you plan to handle a sales proposal for a new client.

Written Document

With the written plan, you create something your boss will read. It's the *product* of your work. You can spend as much or as little time as you want preparing it, because you're going to e-mail it to your boss when you're finished and not before. When your boss receives the report, she reads it. If she has questions, she can ask them, and the questions are in response to the document itself.

Conversation

During the conversation, you and your boss are involved in a *process*. You talk about the new client and what you plan to propose. You ask each other questions to clarify ideas and think through your options. You both speak and you both listen. The conversation may jump from topic to topic in a nonlinear way. That's okay, though, because what the conversation lacks in structure, it makes up for in immediacy and nuance. When you and your boss leave the break room, you have her feedback and support. As with any conversation, you and your boss share a moment in time, and both of you are fully present in that moment.

Now let's break down this comparison by using our three variables.

	Written Documents: A product	Informal Conversations: A process	
Method of Reception	**Reading** Written documents are meant to be read and can be reread as many times as the reader wants.	**Listening** Conversations involve listening to the other participants in the moment.	Method of Reception
Level of Spontaneity	**Low** Documents are written at one point in time and read in another.	**High** During conversations, ideas are conceived and shared immediately.	Level of Spontaneity
Degree of Participation	**Low** Reading is a passive, non-interactive task.	**High** Conversations are an active process, an exchange of information between two or more people.	Degree of Participation

Neither of these types of communication is inherently better than the other, although at times one is more appropriate than the other. The rule of thumb most people follow is that if you have a lot of detailed information to communicate, write it down. If you want to explain the subtleties of that information and make sure that someone understands it, sit down and have a conversation.

Now let's add speeches and presentations to the comparison. Speeches are closer to written documents. Presentations are closer to conversations.

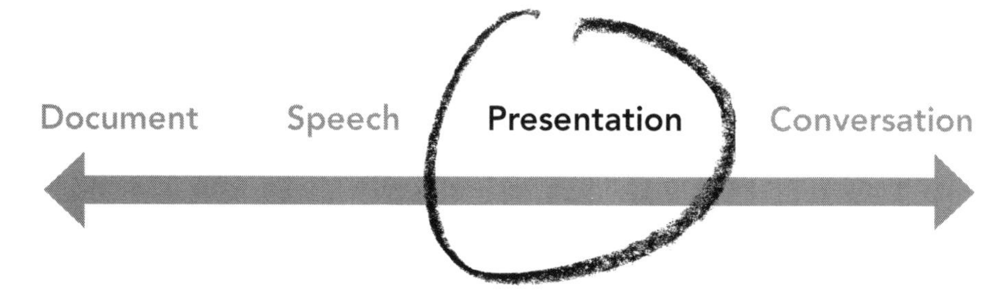

Speeches	Presentations
Method of Reception Audience members listen to the delivery of the script. When speechmakers use slides or other visual support, it is subordinate to what is heard.	**Method of Reception** Audience members receive information by listening to the presenter and by looking at or reading from visuals. Hard copies of the slides are often distributed to the audience. Sometimes the primary message is received by listening, at other times by reading.
Level of Spontaneity Because speeches are performances, they are not spontaneously delivered. They are rehearsed—sometimes memorized, more often read from a printed text or prompter.	**Level of Spontaneity** While speechmakers rehearse to appear spontaneous, a presenter actually is. Business audiences want to feel that this is the first time the presenter has said these things in exactly this way. If they don't, a genuine conversation can't take place. When delivering a presentation, the presenter is in the here and now of the audience. The information that's delivered, though, was prepared at another time and place.
Degree of Participation The audience's role is passive. They may smile, laugh, and nod their heads in agreement, but they do not participate directly until the Q&A session following the speech.	**Degree of Participation** Audience members are active participants, directly or indirectly influencing how information is delivered. During preparation, the presenter's job is to create a framework for the interaction that will take place. During delivery, he or she encourages response from the audience while controlling it enough to keep the process on track.

In an ideal world, this unique combination of characteristics results in a presentation during which (1) everyone stays focused and participates appropriately, (2) the visuals you use are exactly what you need when you need them, (3) your audience never gets lost, and (4) in the end, you reach your goal.

As we all know, though, circumstances are never ideal. During most business presentations (1) it's difficult to hold the attention of the group for an extended period of time; (2) the conversation doesn't always follow the order of the slides, and the slides you have are not always the slides you need; (3) someone, you or an audience member, will always think that a particular topic is receiving too much or too little attention; and (4) the audience will be active and passive, but not exactly when you want them to be.

Just as no other type of communication can accomplish what Orderly Conversations can, no other type of communication requires this combination of planning and flexibility. No wonder presenters struggle.

So What Does This Mean for You?

It's important to understand that presentations are an imperfect, unpredictable process. Once they begin, like all genuine conversations, they take on a life of their own. Your job as presenter is to let the conversation happen without losing sight of your goal. Success requires creating a plan that looks ahead to the uncertainties of delivery. Delivery, in turn, relies

Success requires creating a plan that looks ahead to the uncertainties of delivery. Delivery, in turn, relies on adapting what was planned to what's happening in the moment.

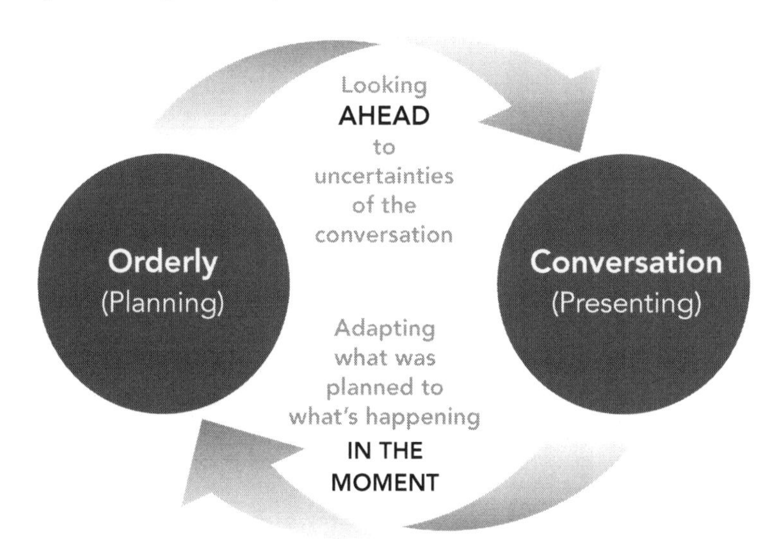

on adapting what was planned to what's happening in the moment.

Throughout the process, on every level, your attention will and should be pulled in both directions—toward the plan and toward the conversation taking place.

This may look like a difficult process, but it's actually much easier than it seems. It requires a clear understanding of what you're planning to do and the conscious application of communication skills you already use.

We'll talk about how that works in the chapters that follow.

Before we go on, let's turn things over to Greg so that he can introduce you to the presenters we'll be working with.

Contents

Chapter 4
Meet the Presenters

In this chapter . . .

- **The Beginning of the Workshop**
- **Here's What the Presenters Have to Say**
- **Initial Analysis**

Greg:

As Dale said in the first chapter, the presenters we'll be writing about face very real issues. Before we hear from each of them, let me provide a little setup. The workshop you will observe is one of our typical two-day classes.

This particular workshop is open to the public, so there is an interesting mix of people. They come from various industries, have a broad range of experience, and bring different skill sets.

Each of the participants has completed some prework and an online needs assessment. The prework is designed to bring each of them to a baseline understanding of what we mean when we talk about Orderly Conversations. The needs assessment gets them thinking about the goals they'd like to achieve during the workshop. It also gives us, the trainers, an introduction to the people and the presentations we'll be working with in class.

As class begins, we facilitate a conversation about the information we received on the assessment. This allows us to dig a little deeper into their responses. We're going to include that discussion here. It will help you understand why people are attending the class, which is important all by itself, but it also will help us see how these presenters think about presenting. That gives us insight into what, if anything, they may need to unlearn.

The Beginning of the Workshop

Imagine the group is seated at a U-shaped table. Dale is standing at the front of the room and starts the session by describing our goals for the training. He explains that we want the participants to be happy they spent two days with us and feel their time was well spent. We also want to work with each of them to identify the unique set of skills and techniques that will help them be more confident, comfortable, and in control of their business presentations.

Dale goes on to talk about the process. The two days are broken down into four experiential modules.

1. **Getting Engaged**
2. **Framing the Conversation**
3. **Presenting the Information**
4. **Managing Interactions**

Each module will include some up-front teaching from us and be followed by experiential exercises. During the exercises, participants practice in front of the group, receive feedback, and try out new skills. We record each exercise on video and follow up with private coaching. This process helps presenters learn on multiple levels. They learn by listening and doing, by providing feedback to one another, and through individual coaching.

I can't stress enough how important the video coaching is. Of course, no one enjoys seeing or hearing themselves on video, but eventually presenters are able to see themselves objectively and identify what they're already doing well. From there, we're able to assess areas in need of improvement.

This video review process also helps people think critically about the task of delivering business presentations. They'll learn that there isn't one right way to present and that everyone takes a different path to success.

Before any of that happens, though, we need to get to know each of the participants. After all, to help them be more successful communicators, we need to understand their situations in more detail, what's led them to the class, and what they'd like to take away.

Here's What the Presenters Have to Say

I work at BakleTech. I am the Director of IT. We are the biggest company you've never heard of. We basically manufacture the stuff that technology products live in. Laptop housings, server racks, and so on. So while it seems that we're an IT company, we're really a manufacturing company. That said, I handle our IT needs as they apply to running the business.

This is the second presentation skills workshop I've taken. The first one was several years ago when I worked at a different company.

I was recently promoted to this position, and it has come with a lot of new responsibilities. Now, I'm primarily a manager of people. Over the past few years, I've moved away from actually working with technology to managing the people who do.

> Terry is in his early 40s and has a medium build and a receding hairline. He's dressed in khakis, a button-down shirt, and a jacket. Meeting him for the first time, you wouldn't be surprised that he works in IT. He's serious and focused when he talks about his job, but his face lights up when he talks about his wife and newborn daughter.

But that's not my issue. My biggest challenge is communicating up the chain to executive leadership. I feel like I don't fit in. The VP of Sales completely freaks me out. When he's in the room I become self-conscious, and words start flying out of my mouth but nothing comes out right. I feel like I can't even get my subjects and verbs to agree. It's bad.

The morning I signed up for this class was a nightmare. I was in a meeting with the senior execs. I was presenting my budget report (which was not good news), and they asked me a question that was technologically complex. I started my answer by giving some background, which I felt was necessary. Apparently I went on too long because a few minutes into it, that guy, the VP of Sales, tossed his pen and said, "We asked you what time it is, not how to build a clock. Just bottom line it."

That was a bad day. I was humiliated. I went directly to my office and searched for a class, and this one is the first that came up. I need a way to deal with this new nervousness and to be more concise.

Another thing—I never know how to prepare. What's the best way? I have a big presentation coming up and I need it to go well.

Oh, and I never know what to do with my hands. The last class I took, the instructor told us to hold our hands at our sides and never gesture unless it was to emphasize a point. I do it because that's the rule, but standing like that feels awkward.

The other thing is that I never know how to get the presentation started. That feels awkward too until I'm a few minutes into it. Then things usually feel okay.

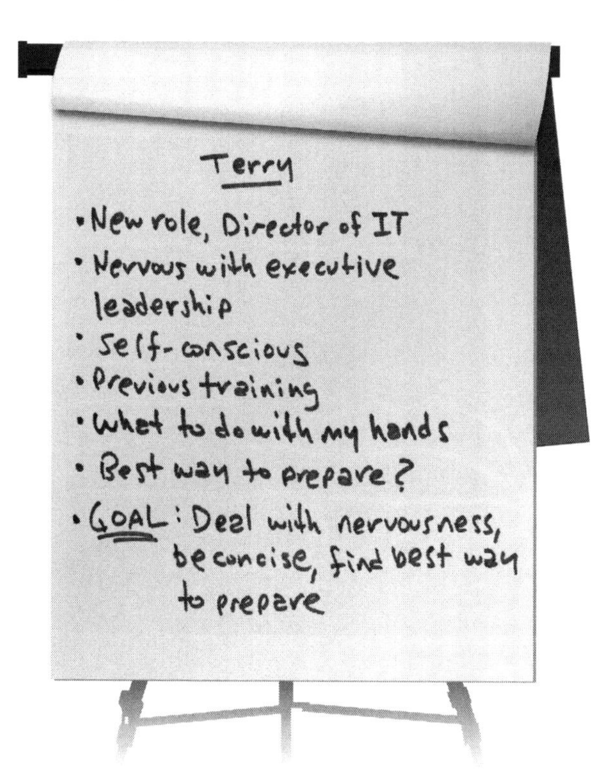

Dorothy

I'm a Regional Manager in the Market Research department at AWR. We make roofing materials for residential use across the country. We're a big company, so you might have our shingles on your house. You can find our products at all of the big-box home improvement stores. Our buyer would be the manager in charge of construction materials at the big box.

Dorothy is probably in her 50s and has a warm, melodic voice. Dressed in a classic brown tweed suit and suede shoes, she looks completely put together. She was the first to arrive and introduced herself to everyone entering the room. She jokes about being vertically challenged.

My job is to take the marketing data we collect and make it useful for the salespeople. We collect all sorts of data about who the consumers are, what they're buying, where they're buying, and why. We measure the effectiveness of sales and promotions. We also keep an eye on the competition to see what they're up to. We're known as a top-quality supplier, so we're very sensitive to what the lower-priced guys are doing to go after our market share.

All of my presentations are internal. I never talk to the actual buyers, just the people who are selling to them. As I said, I try to make the data useful to them. The problem is that there's a lot of it, and they don't always fully understand it. This means if they show the data to their buyers, they probably aren't using it very well.

To solve this problem, we set up monthly market research meetings with the salespeople. I work in the central region office, so I just meet with the people from there, not the whole organization. I focus my meetings on what's happening in the region. I talk about how the region is doing overall, what's working well, what's not working so well. One of my frustrations is that these meetings tend to go in all sorts of directions. They can be chaotic, and people ask questions about things I've already talked about. I know it would be rude to say this, but I just want to scream, "I already talked about that. If you were paying attention, you'd know that!" What's the best way to deal with that?

To make things worse, some of the salespeople attend virtually.

So my goal in this workshop is to make my presentations more interesting and practical. I work really hard preparing for each one of them, but the feedback I've received is that I'm too detailed and that the salespeople think the meetings are a waste of time.

Also, I suspect they don't use the slides I give them. So I'd like some advice on that too.

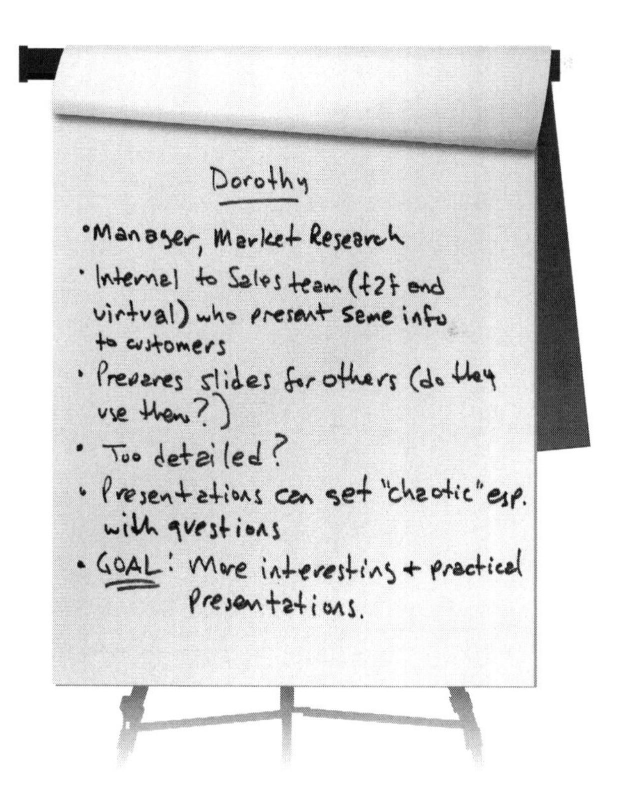

Michael

I'm an Account Manager at NHS, which stands for Nalley Health Systems. You've probably heard of our diet plan that's been around for about 20 years. About five years ago, we started selling products through retail outlets. Basically, it was a logical step to take advantage of our brand and reputation in a new channel.

My focus is on energy bars and meal-replacement bars. My job is to persuade buyers at major food chains to put them on their shelves.

Basically, the company is doing well; although, as you can guess, the competition is fierce. The sales presentations I deliver are usually done across the desk with a single buyer. The buyers are always busy and distracted. Sometimes other people are in the room, like the category manager or the assistant buyer, but my job is really focused on persuading the buyer. If I get the buy-in of anyone else in the room, that's secondary.

Michael looks like a runner or a tennis player. He's in shape, self-confident, and his clothes are freshly pressed. It was no surprise to anyone that he works for a health food company. He carries his laptop in a backpack with his company's logo on it.

These meetings are pretty informal, and sometimes I feel like the buyer is in charge, not me. I always take in a hard copy of a slide deck that I try to at least talk about a little bit. It's mostly meant to be left behind. It has information about products, in-store displays, new product innovations, and so on. The slides also include the customer's sales figures from the last quarter. Sometimes the sales numbers are the focus of the entire meeting.

I usually have some samples with me.

What I want to work on in this class is getting to the close. I've known this one particular buyer at Super-Market for a long time. She doesn't give me much time. Usually only 15 minutes. When I walk in the door, we typically start chatting about what's new and how her kids are doing in gymnastics. She has two really talented daughters. I feel like I get all caught up in the conversation with her and never really accomplish the task at hand. Lately, I've had to wrap things up through e-mail or a phone call after the meeting. I'd like to get things done while I'm in the office with her.

The other thing I'd like to talk about is a situation that comes up all the time. It's happened twice in recent visits. I sit down and immediately get thrown a curve ball. One time, a buyer was upset about an out-of-stock issue from the warehouse that I wasn't even aware of. Another time this guy was peeved about a competitor having better pricing in their circular. It's not so much that I disagree with their frustration; I just don't know how to handle it in the moment. It's as if the temperature in the room goes from 70 degrees to 95.

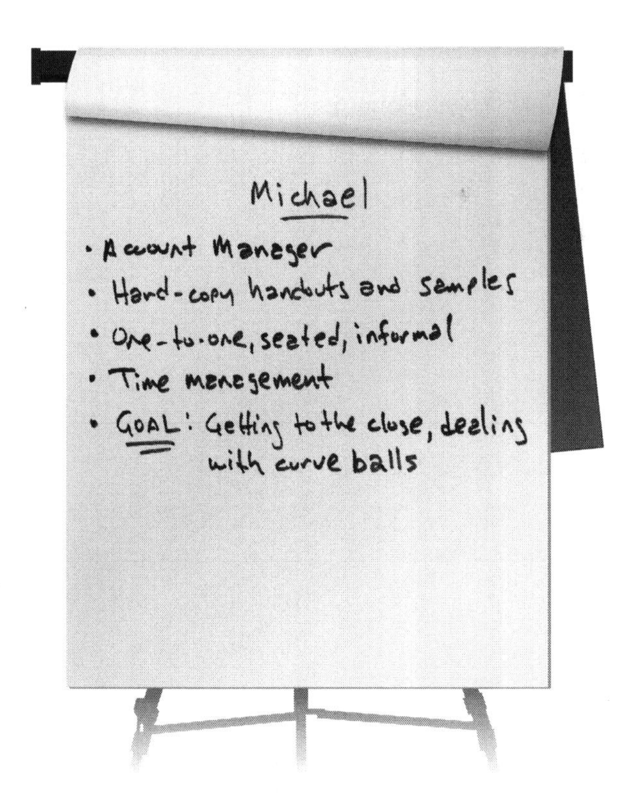

I am a coordinator in the accounting department of a law firm called Mitchell & Montgomery. I've been in my current position for only three months. I was promoted from a more administrative role. I had that job for two years. Before that, I was in college earning a degree in business.

At first, Jennifer seems quiet and reserved. She's slight, in her mid-20s, and wearing a stylish gray suit. Her hair is pulled back off her face. Although she doesn't command the most attention in the room, she's a good listener and empathizes with the others as they talk about being a little anxious about this training.

My old boss considered me a high-potential employee and worked really hard to find me the right job at the firm. I like being in accounting except for one thing—the presentations I have to do. My fiancé suggested I take this course. I think he's tired of hearing me whine about presenting. So, that's why I'm here.

I get really nervous. I'm even nervous right now. I'm shaking like a leaf!

Whenever I get asked a question, I freeze. It's not that I don't know the answer, but it pulls me off script and I can't deal with it.

My new boss is gradually getting me involved in our monthly department meetings. The whole department gets together to talk about the projects we're working on and the quarterly reports we'll send out to the partners at the firm.

At our next meeting, I'll be doing a presentation about our new reimbursement process. I know that the process itself is a good one because when I was an admin, I was on the committee that helped design it. The presentation is pretty much ready to go. I just have a few more adjustments to make.

The thing is, I'm just terrified about presenting it to anyone. I get so nervous I can hardly get a word out. The last presentation I delivered at one of these monthly meetings was a disaster. I practiced several times, but it wasn't enough.

My goal for this workshop is to find a cure for the anxiety.

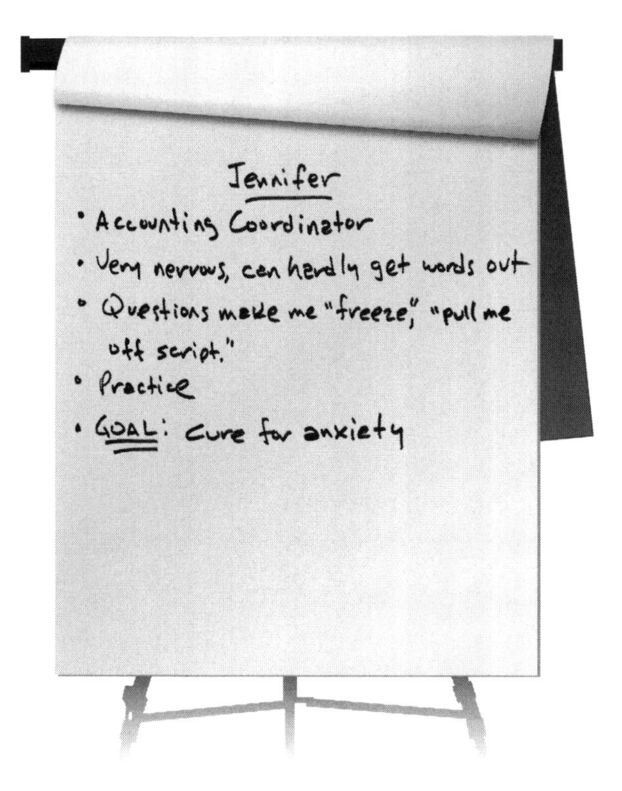

JAMES

I am the President of Jones & Harvey. I founded the company 30 years ago with Henry Jones. He up and retired a couple years ago, but the company still has his name. I thought about changing it, but why bother. It is what it is.

Henry and I met when we both worked for a big electronics company. We were engineers, and what we had in common was that we both hated our jobs. We used to sit around and talk about finding work that was better suited to our personalities. Something less stuffy and corporate.

> James, who is probably in his late 50s, is a little intimidating. He has a deep, gruff voice that matches his physical appearance. With his buzz cut, you might expect him to be in the military. When he and Dorothy met, she said, "Goodness, that's a firm handshake you have there."

We found it, but not in the way we thought. What happened was that we were asked to figure out how to protect sensitive products during shipping. It started out as a little project. What we developed is a system that uses special materials and die-cut forms that will protect just about anything you choose to put in it. We thought it was a great idea and wanted to develop it further. The electronics company wasn't interested in pursuing this line of business, so we left and started our own company. We had our old company's blessings, of course, and they became our first big customer.

What I do now is run the company. We're still pretty small with under a hundred employees. Henry used to be in charge of sales, so when he retired we had to hire someone to do it. My job is not to manage the client relationship per se, but rather to be the figurehead when we're doing a sales presentation to potential customers, especially the big, important ones.

The reason I'm in this workshop is that the new VP of Sales, her name is

Kim, has told me that I tend to dominate the presentations a bit. According to her, I say too much and wind up stepping on people's toes. She also says I talk about things that aren't relevant to where we are in the sales cycle. According to her, I come off as disorganized. I never had this problem with Henry. We knew each other so well we could finish each other's sentences.

But times change. And maybe this old dog needs to learn a few new tricks. At least that's what my wife says.

I've been doing this for so long that I don't experience any nervousness, never did really. I don't even prepare that much. Kim has put together some new slides for me to use, so I try to use them. But to be honest, I don't need a slide to talk about the company. And besides, her slides are too . . . something. What's the word? She animates them, which I find annoying. I'd rather just talk and answer questions. That's a better way to build relationships.

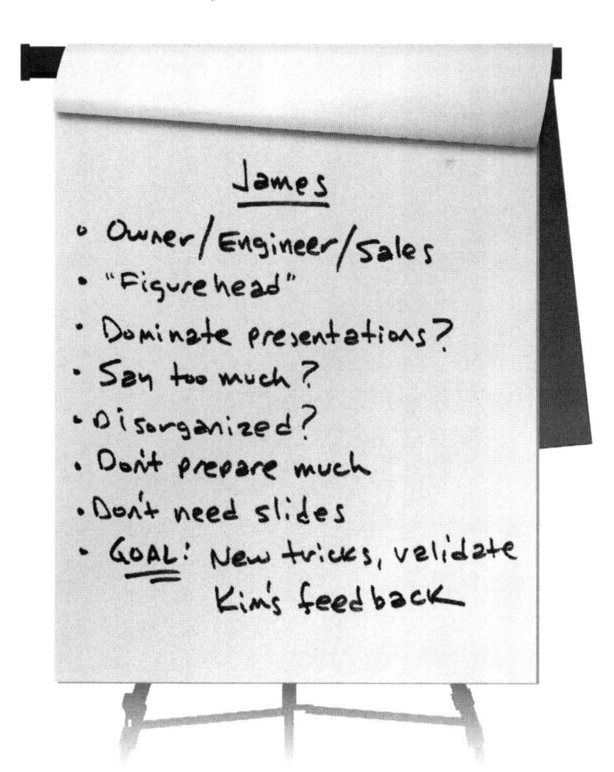

Sophia

I'm a Senior Trainer at Westward Credit Union. I've been in Learning & Development for most of my career, about 15 years now. I've worked at Westward for seven of those years. My job? I love it and I truly enjoy delivering training. I have always enjoyed being in front of people, even when I was little. I think the key to my success is being prepared and energetic. People always describe me as passionate on workshop evaluations.

I practice a lot before each training session. I had a boss tell me once that when you're training adults, it's important to go in with a solid plan and really sell it to the people in the class. So that's what I try to do. I mean I'm not trying to push anything down their throats, but I try to make it interesting and fun for everyone. There needs to be a little pizzazz in every trainer, I believe.

In her late 30s, Sophia is casually dressed in slacks and a loose-fitting sweater. She is energetic and speaks quickly. She and Jennifer struck up a conversation as they ate breakfast. They agreed that the cantaloupe was delicious and that the honeydew was (as usual) tasteless.

My goal for this training? Practice delivering an upcoming initiative. My current manager thought my skills could use some polishing. I suppose she's right. I definitely need to explore some ways I can get buy-in quickly for this training session because there will be resistance, I'm sure. Maybe you can suggest a good icebreaker that will help me gain the buy-in?

I know once I do that, I'll be able to deliver the information. I've been a trainer for so long that I really don't get very nervous anymore. Sometimes, though, when the learners get restless, it bothers me. But I try to go in with a positive attitude and get everybody excited about the class.

People sometimes say I speak too fast. When I practice, that's one of the things I work on.

Oh, and something else? There are two specific people that I just know are going to be a pain. They've been around a long time, and they resist everything. The real problem is that they influence everyone around them. I'd like to get your advice for nipping their negativity in the bud. I feel that if I can just shut them down early, things will go more smoothly for me.

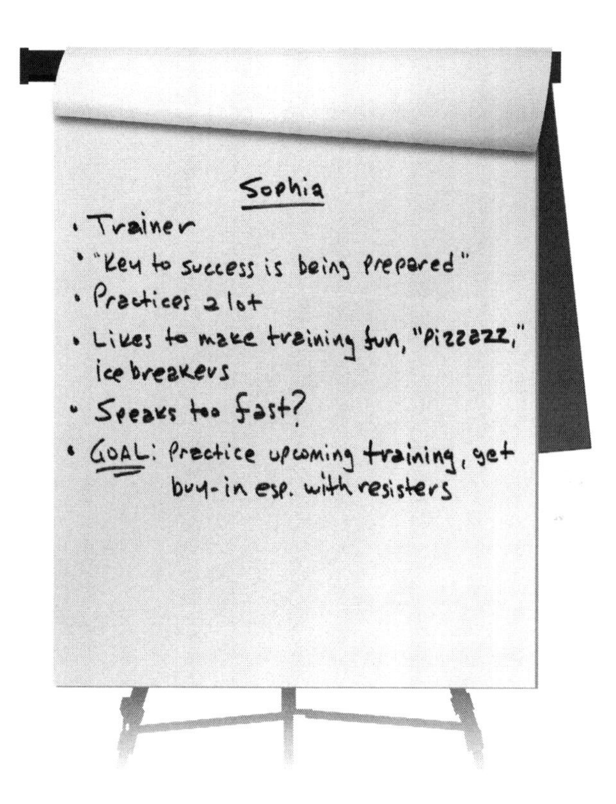

I'm the founder of 14 Ways, a technology start-up that was actually a class project in grad school. Two of my classmates are still involved. One is the Chief Technology Officer and the other is the Chief Marketing Officer. We're about 24 months into it, and things are going well. Sales are good, but it's time for some serious funding so that we can go to the next level.

That's what I'll be working on in class, our pitch to a VC (that's venture capitalist). The last time we delivered an important presentation, I was horrible. The other two were not great, but I was downright bad. We were presenting to an entrepreneurial incubator group. It was a contest for start-up funding. It did not go well. I blathered on and on, and the audience just stared back at me. It was really odd. We didn't win.

The first thing you notice about Luis is that he seems too young to be in this workshop. If you had to guess, you'd probably say he was 21 years old. He wears thick-rimmed glasses and has dark wavy hair. He's soft-spoken and seems a little nervous. But he is comfortable chatting with everyone in the room, even James.

After that, I knew I needed a class to get me ready. All three of us took a public speaking course in undergrad, and we had to present all the time in grad school. But those were different from this, and the stakes are much higher now.

I read *The Art of the Start* by Guy Kawasaki, so I understand his very practical recommendations and what's expected of us. We just need to be able to do it. What I like about his book is that he doesn't sugarcoat entrepreneurialism. It's hard, and he says so. But he also lays out—very clearly—the things you need to do in practical terms to create the environment for success. Communicating clearly and succinctly to VCs is one of them.

The problem for me is that my head is all over the place when I present. It's not that I'm overly nervous; my thoughts are just jumbled and swirling around. I'm sure that makes me come off as flaky and unprofessional. The VCs want to know that I can focus, manage huge sums of money, and build the company into a viable organization. I need to project that image to them. Right now, I'm not able to do that because I talk in circles and don't know how or when to stop.

Also, I look young for my age, and I think that works against me. Is there anything I can do to appear more mature?

I'm a Community Liaison for a large construction company. I'm in the residential group, and I'm the lucky one who has to present at town hall meetings and convince them that putting up a condo in their neighborhood is a good idea. It usually isn't that big of an issue, but there are times, especially when we're asking them to rezone an area, when it becomes a zoo. Community activists can get very worked up about these things, especially when it comes to nature preservation or modernizing historic neighborhoods.

> Elaine is in her mid-40s, tall and slender. When she walks in the room, your first thought would be that no matter what she does for a living, she's good at it. She's friendly and eager to get to know everyone in the group. She carries a beautiful briefcase.

I'm here to learn how to manage my presentations when things turn hostile. I know it's not personal, and it has nothing to do with me, but I turn into mush when people interrupt and yell at me. It's like my brain just shuts down, so Jennifer, I can relate to what you described when people ask you questions. And, like you, Terry, I'm not anxious, unless people get rude. I can't believe that guy tossed his pen! I would have melted.

People always say how confident I appear. But at these meetings, things change.

I've seen my boss present at these things, and she's great. It doesn't seem to bother her at all. I want to be like her—calm, cool, reserved. It's as if she can detach and become someone else.

Oh, something else. I get the sense that everyone here projects slides on a screen, except maybe you, Michael. I will sometimes project a virtual tour if the room setup will allow for that, but I usually use posters, models, and maybe some brochures. I hope that's okay.

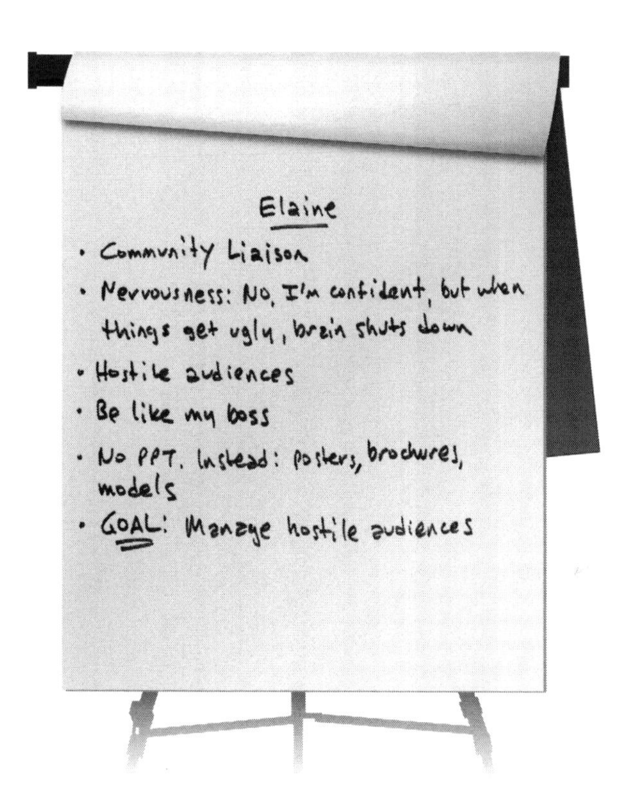

Initial Analysis

There they are, our eight class participants. On one hand, they're a very typical group. On the other hand, as you can see, each has a unique set of issues he or she needs to address.

Nervousness affects several of them, but it manifests itself differently in each. For example, Jennifer freezes and can "hardly get a word out." Terry can't stop talking even though he fears he's not making sense.

Luis, James, and Dorothy are on the other side of the spectrum. They don't experience a lot of nervousness, but based on what we've heard so far, they may lack the flexibility required to be successful presenters.

Some of the presenters, whether they recognize it or not, could benefit from adjusting how they think about presenting. For example,

- Terry follows rules about gestures that he was taught in a previous training session, even though doing so makes him feel awkward.
- Sophia feels that training has to be entertaining to be effective. This assumption, as we'll soon find out, is causing problems for her.
- Elaine wants to present like her boss.
- Jennifer thinks she needs to memorize and practice until she feels ready. Unfortunately, this approach hasn't worked for her.

Moving forward, you will look in as these eight presenters participate in the workshop. You will relate to some more than others, so you may want to follow those people more closely. As you do, you will learn from their learning and find ways to apply these concepts to yourself and your own Orderly Conversations.

Contents

Chapter 5
Stop Performing

In this chapter . . .

- **How We Got Here: Getting Past Public Speaking 101**
- **Three Types of Performers**
- **Surprising Support**
- **So What Does This Mean for You?**

Dale:

As we said in Chapter 2, approaching your presentations as a performance prevents a genuine conversation between presenter and audience. In this chapter, we'll talk more specifically about that. We'll look at two things: how well-intentioned presenters typically apply the performance approach, and how that approach increases nervousness.

The lure of the performance approach is control. Presenters use it because they assume success comes from planning exactly what they are going to say and how they will say it in advance of the presentation. This also means, their thinking goes, that success can be reached fairly easily because all they have to do is remember the plan and follow the rules.

The danger is that exercising this level of control over the process pulls your focus away from the here and now of the conversation and leads, for many people, to increased nervousness.

How We Got Here: Getting Past Public Speaking 101

Most people were introduced to the performance approach in school.

It is the method used in public speaking courses taught in high school and college. This class goes by many names, but for the sake of simplicity, I'll refer to it as 101. To be fair to those who teach this kind of class, as I did early in my career, it is a class *about* public speaking. It is not designed to make every student a polished speechmaker or a successful business presenter.

You probably remember that 101 focuses on the fundamental steps required to prepare and deliver three or four speeches. Students learn about audience analysis, research, outlining, and delivery. Grades are determined by how well students manage each of these processes. The final step, the delivery of the speech, is assessed through the use of an evaluation form, a checklist used to grade the speech. That's the part of the process I want to focus on now.

The delivery section of the evaluation form is typically broken down into subcategories—vocal variety, rate, articulation, eye contact, posture, enthusiasm, gestures, and so on. During each speech these behaviors are rated, usually with a numerical value. The good thing about this process is that students know exactly what's expected of them. It also helps the instructor grade each student fairly and efficiently using the same set of standards.

The bad thing, though, is that this type of evaluation leads to prescriptive rules and standardized behavior. Even if the rules attempt to solve real problems and encourage good outcomes, they are still rules—unexamined and generic.

Here are some of the 101-style rules presenters have brought into our workshops.

1. Eliminate all filler words.
2. Be sure to start with a higher than usual level of enthusiasm.
3. Leave your hands at your sides, because gestures are distracting.

4. When you begin your presentation, walk to a specific spot in the room and stand there for a specific length of time.
5. Look at people around the room, but if you're uncomfortable, don't look them in the eye.
6. Never turn your back on the audience.
7. Never read from your slides.
8. When you need to refer to your slides, look at your laptop monitor.
9. Memorize the opening.
10. The granddaddy of them all: Practice makes perfect.

When rules like these are applied without consideration of their effectiveness or appropriateness for an individual, they stop being the means to an end and become the end themselves. This makes presenting more difficult for the presenter and less effective for the audience.

Three Types of Performers

Business presenters who follow a performance approach generally fall into three categories: the Dutiful Student, the Entertainer, and the Nervous Perfectionist.

The Dutiful Student

Many presenters simply crave the simplicity and comfort of rules. Dutiful Students ask, "What's the rule about gestures?" "Where's the right place to stand?" They wonder how many seconds a pause should last or whether to direct eye contact from left to right or right to left. While these presenters are only

It's never a good idea to *begin* with a rule. If you do, you're focusing on the *appearance* of good delivery and not the *effect* of it.

trying to do what it takes to succeed, their focus on rules pulls them away from the decisions they should naturally make during a presentation.

Often, a Dutiful Student will challenge us on our stance on one-size-fits-all rules. After all, their thinking goes, following rules is simple. "Besides," they argue, "you have to agree that there are better and worse ways to do things." Our response to this is, yes, there are better and worse ways to do things. But it's never a good idea to *begin* with a rule. If you do, you're focusing on the *appearance* of good delivery and not the *effect* of it.

Our Dutiful Student

In looking at our workshop participants, we know that Terry, the Director of IT, is our Dutiful Student. His instinct is to seek rules and follow them. Remember, he asked about the rule for where his hands should go and for the best way to prepare.

Following formulaic rules may have served him well as a programmer sitting at his desk getting the code just right. But things are different now that he's a member of the leadership team. His ability to communicate more effectively is central to his role and how successful he'll be in it.

Dutiful Students need to understand that successful delivery is a response to what's happening with the audience right now. The presenter's primary goal is to do whatever it takes to stay in the moment. Rules get in the way of that.

The Entertainer

Like Dutiful Students, Entertainers want predictability and control, but they aren't necessarily interested in rules. They usually have excellent control over their voices and bodies and enjoy being in front of an audience. They often say they want

Instead of focusing on making what they say relevant and useful, Entertainers focus on delivering it perfectly.

their presentations to be fun. While this may sound like a good thing, maybe even an enviable thing, it's a red flag for us. I'm always dubious when presenters talk about making things fun. It reminds me of jokes told badly and pointless group activities.

Some Entertainers have had acting or some other performance background, so their attempt to transfer those skills to their presentations is understandable. The problem, though, is that the meeting room is not a stage. When Entertainers perform, the fourth wall springs up, and audience members become observers and sometimes not very willing observers. This effect leads to Entertainers seeming unaware, insincere, or unapproachable.

Our Entertainer

We can easily see that Sophia, the trainer, is the Entertainer of the group. She talked about adding pizzazz and making her training fun for everyone.

While some of her audience members may appreciate her efforts, others won't. Her performance approach may cause them to tune her out, which will mean wasted time and will ultimately prevent her from reaching her goals.

Too often, the Entertainer's need to add excitement to the process is an attempt to make the presentation palatable for the audience. Instead of focusing on making what they say relevant and useful, Entertainers focus on delivering it perfectly. It's a little like spending more energy wrapping a gift than making sure the gift is something the receiver actually wants.

I'm not saying we want to banish humor and fun from the process. It's just that both need to spring from what's happening in the moment. They should not be overly planned or pasted on.

The Nervous Perfectionist

By far, the most common application of the performance approach is found with Nervous Perfectionists. This type of presenter uses performance techniques—especially rehearsal—to perfect the presentation. The Nervous Perfectionist's goal in doing this is to prevent nervousness. This idea appears in virtually every book on public speaking. It's the unwavering, unchallenged notion that "practice makes perfect."

As logical as it may seem, this approach works only with speechmakers. To understand what we mean, let's take a closer look at how Jennifer described the first presentation she delivered in her new job.

I have always been nervous when I speak in front of a group of people. It's not that I'm shy. I just feel foolish if I stumble over my words or lose my train of thought. In my new job, I have to deliver presentations about once a month. They're not to clients or any of the attorneys at the firm, which I would never be able to do. They're just to the other people in accounting, and that includes my boss, of course.

So when it was time for my first presentation, I was completely prepared. My slides were ready as soon as I received the data I needed. I went into the meeting room the day before the presentation to rehearse. I talked through my presentation three times. I memorized the opening sentences, planned where to stand, made adjustments to my slides, and really worked on my transitions and enthusiasm. When I went home that night, I felt pretty good about things, but I practiced one last time with my fiancé.

The next day I was nervous, but not too bad. I mean, I knew what I wanted to say, and I knew everyone in the room. They really are nice people. So when it was my turn, I walked to the front of the room, brought up my first slide, and began. My mouth was dry, but I think I got through the part that I memorized just fine.

Then I stumbled on the third slide. It was so silly. Instead of saying that the team had made excellent progress in the past month, I said they had made *excellence* progress or something like that. I tried to correct it but got tied up in all the "S" sounds. Then I started feeling really warm and couldn't remember what I was trying to say. From that point on, I don't even remember what I did. I got through my slides, but I went really fast. I'm sure I forgot all of my transitions. At the end, it was so embarrassing. I said something like, "Well I guess that's it." I didn't even use my conclusion slide.

Our Nervous Perfectionist

It's clear that Jennifer is our Nervous Perfectionist. Like other people of this type, she assumes that success stems from memorizing what she plans to say.

While this may seem reasonable, it prevents her from connecting with the other people involved in the conversation.

After the meeting, my boss told me that my data was good and that presenting it would get easier with time. Then he said, "At least you went so fast that we finished the meeting early." Not exactly the comment I had hoped for. Next time, I'll have to start rehearsing two days before.

Challenges for the Nervous Perfectionist

What happened to Jennifer happens to a lot of presenters. By assuming that performance techniques like memorization and rehearsal would give her the control she wanted, she lost sight of the process. She didn't realize that besides affecting her connection with the audience, her approach increased her discomfort and prevented her from reaching her goals.

Her assumptions look like this.

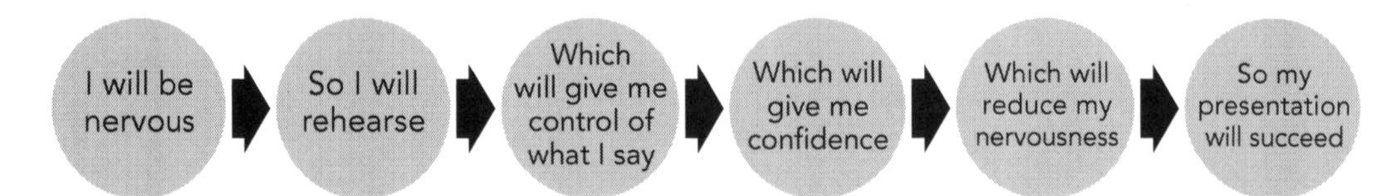

As Jennifer moved through each of these steps, she assumed she was gradually taking control over the process. But it didn't work. What happened to Jennifer actually looks like this.

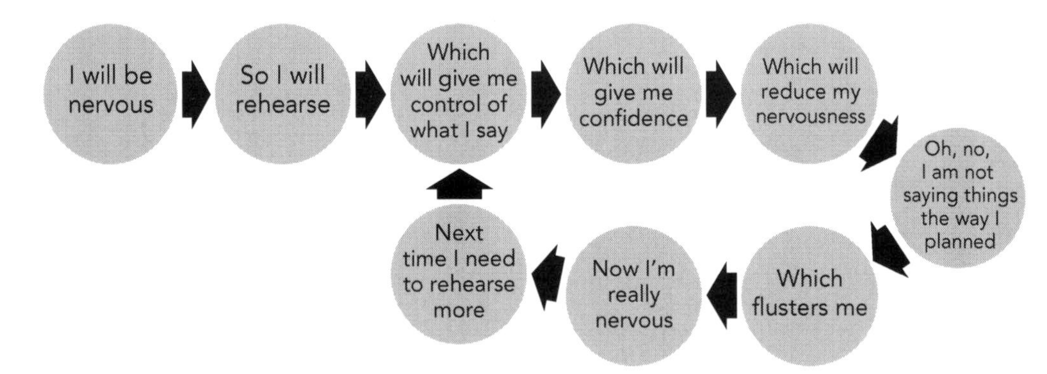

As you can see, Jennifer's nervousness led her to rehearse, which turned her presentation into a performance. This made her more self-conscious and more nervous. Her decision to rehearse more for the next presentation just repeats the cycle.

Nervous Perfectionists relax not only *when* they engage their listeners in a conversation, but *because* they have done so.

Nervous Perfectionists relax not only *when* they engage their listeners in a conversation, but *because* they have done so. The best thing they can do to manage their nervousness is to focus on the audience and lose their faith in rehearsal.

Not every presenter falls as neatly into these three categories as Terry, Sophia, and Jennifer do, of course. You may see yourself in more than one of them. Use the categories to help you dig beneath surface behaviors to the deeper attitudes and assumptions driving you.

Surprising Support

During the early stages of writing this book, I was surprised and pleased to meet Richard Doetkott, a professor of Communication Studies at Chapman University. Doetkott taught the 101 course at that school. We met at a conference where he was delivering a short talk about how he had drastically reduced the stage fright students experienced in his classes. He had done so by rejecting the traditional methodology and replacing it with what he calls a "conversing" approach.

Although it had been years since I taught 101, what Doetkott had to say resonated deeply. No one else at the conference approached the process in the way that he did.

At the time of his talk, Doetkott had just completed a 101 textbook. In it, he says traditional 101 courses encourage performance. As he puts it, "[In a typical 101 class] students are required to practice . . . their gestures, voice, facial expressions, etc. . . . What this amounts to is the teaching of *acting.*" He goes on to make the important connection between performance and nervousness. "Performing is the same whether on the stage or at the Olympics or in the traditional [public speaking] classroom. It is unnatural, stressful and produces *stage fright.* Every time."[1]

In Doetkott's classes, then, students are encouraged to abandon conventions of delivery and converse with their audience. When they do, his research shows, they can significantly reduce their nervousness. I was excited that Doetkott was providing evidence supporting something my team and I have observed with nervous presenters for years.

After the conference, I exchanged several e-mails with Doetkott in an effort to dig a little further into his work and sources. I learned

---

1. R. Doetkott, L. Lockwood, and P. Doetkott, *Introduction to Public Conversing* (Charlotte, NC: Kona Publishing and Media Group, 2011), 28.

that Doetkott builds his case, in part, on the work of James McCroskey at the University of Alabama–Birmingham. McCroskey says that nervousness is the result of a presenter's self-centeredness.

If McCroskey had seen Jennifer struggle with her nervousness, he would have said she is overly concerned with the externals. She is thinking about how she looks and sounds as she speaks. Her internal focus prevents her from thinking about what she is communicating to the audience and whether they were "getting the idea (she) wants them to get."[2]

Both McCroskey and Doetkott would say Jennifer should turn her attention away from herself and what she rehearsed and direct it toward the audience she is addressing. It's the same process we recommend for all presenters, even those who do not suffer from debilitating nervousness.

So What Does This Mean for You?

The fundamental issue is not what you look and sound like, nor is it what you do to prevent nervousness. Rather, it is this: how do you engage listeners in the conversation in a way that reduces your nervousness?

That topic will be the focus of the next chapter, in which I'll talk a bit more about Doetkott and another of the academics he directed me toward.

2. James C. McCroskey, *An Introduction to Rhetorical Communication* (Boston: Allyn & Bacon, 1997), 270.

Contents

Chapter 6
Get Engaged

In this chapter . . .

- **Trapped in the Funhouse**
- **Engagement Is about the Most Fundamental Skills**
- **The Power of Eye Contact and Pausing**
- **Making These Skills Work for You**
- **The Engagement Exercise**
- **So What Does This Mean for You?**

Most of the presenters we work with describe the beginning of their presentations in the same way. They say they feel okay once they "get over the hump" or "get in the flow" of the presentation. When they describe this process, what they're talking about is getting engaged in the conversation. Getting over the hump, as McCroskey would say, means focusing on the audience and bringing them into the conversation. At the beginning of every presentation, it's your job to make this happen.

Sometimes reaching a solid level of engagement takes a while. This might be the result of the presenter's nervousness. It might be because the presenter hasn't quite made the transition from thinking about what he or she wants to say and actually saying it.

The thing to remember is that at the beginning of every presentation, it's your job to move from disengagement to engagement. The transition between the two is often a little uncomfortable.

Trapped in the Funhouse

Moving from disengagement to engagement is a lot like what you experience in a carnival funhouse. If you've ever been in one, you know funhouses usually have a hall of mirrors and a room with tilting floors. As you move through, you laugh at your distorted image in the mirrors and stumble as the floor moves beneath you. When you are nervous and disengaged at the beginning of your presentations, you experience a similar level of disorientation, but it's not fun. When you're in *this* funhouse, you feel distracted, uncomfortable, and unsure of yourself.

The first time I was in a real funhouse, I was a kid. I remember the exit was just beyond a spinning barrel. This was the type of barrel that, if you were tall and strong enough, you could plant your feet and hands on the wall, hold yourself in place, and spin around 360 degrees. I was too little for that, so all I could do was walk through the barrel as it slowly turned. To do that, I had to focus on the exit and ignore the fact that the floor was moving. It took a lot more effort and concentration than I had expected.

What presenters need to do is very much like that. It's just that your exit from the funhouse is through the connection you make with your audience. As you're beginning your presentation and getting your footing, you need to focus on individuals in the audience, think about what you want to say to them, and engage them in the conversation. Just like getting through the spinning barrel, it's harder than it looks.

James Winans is one of the scholars Doetkott quotes in his text. Winans says that when you're engaged in a conversation, your mental state has these two qualities: "full realization of the content of your words as you utter them" and "a lively sense of communication." In other words, a conversation requires spontaneity and focus on the other people involved. Winans was writing in 1915, and he's still right.[3]

---

3. James Albert Winans, *Public Speaking: Principles and Practice* (Ithaca, NY: Sewell Publishing, 1915), 28.

The challenge is in knowing how to meet Winans's requirements for engagement when you're nervous or distracted. Before we go further, let me clarify the distinction between an *engaging* presenter and an *engaged* one. An engaging presenter is charming. An engaged presenter is grounded, focused, and in the moment. This is the type of presenter we're interested in here.

An engaged presenter is grounded, focused, and in the moment.

Engagement Is about the Most Fundamental Skills

Engaging your listeners requires the conscious use of eye contact and pausing: eye contact to connect with listeners, pausing to think about what you're saying. We refer to these as engagement skills. As I write this, I hear Doetkott's warning that the *conscious* use of any delivery skill can lead to trouble because it pulls the presenter out of the moment and into performance mode. When that happens, presenters start thinking about the skill and not what the skill is supposed to do.

This may be true, at least temporarily, but it is also true that when you're in the funhouse, you're in a Catch-22. Because you're disengaged, you resist eye contact, but you can't engage until you make eye contact. The same is true for pausing. When you're standing at the front of the room, your mind can be so overwhelmed with racing thoughts and worries that it's nearly impossible to pause, even to take a breath. But you won't stop the racing until you stop—and think. We've all seen presenters stuck in this situation. So with all due respect to Doetkott, there are times when it's appropriate to take conscious control of these skills.

Just keep in mind that we are not talking about eye contact and pausing as elements of a performance. It's not about how your eye contact makes you appear to the audience or the dramatic effect of your pauses. We're talking about using these skills to initiate and engage in the conversation.

The Power of Eye Contact and Pausing

If you step out of the world of presenting for a minute, you can see how the conscious use of these skills works in other stressful situations. For example, think back to when you were a child and something exciting happened at school—maybe you got a higher than expected grade or won a contest. After school, you ran in the house to tell someone about it. Let's say your grandmother was watching you that day. You came in, talking fast, blurting out your story in a way that was impossible for her to understand. Your grandmother might have said, "Slow down. I can't understand you. Stop. Breathe. Now tell me what happened." You forced yourself to stop. You took a breath. You told her what happened.

The same is true with eye contact. Suppose it's another school day, and your grandmother is watching you again. Earlier in the day, you got in a scuffle on the playground and ripped your jacket. As you walk into the house, you hope your grandmother won't notice the tear. If she does you'll have to explain what happened and, truth be told, you started the scuffle. Grandmother notices the rip in the jacket, of course, and asks what happened. After you make a few feeble attempts to circumvent the truth, which you knew wouldn't work anyway, your grandmother says, "Okay, let's get to the truth of the situation. I want you to stand right here, look me in the eye, and tell me what happened on the playground today. Take your time. I'm ready to listen." This is, of course, the worst thing that could happen because you know there is no way around the truth when you're looking your grandmother in the eye. She's got you where she wants you, and you have no choice but to tell the whole story.

In both of these situations, you had a conversation with your grandmother. Both conversations were achieved by focusing on a skill that helped you engage. Neither skill was easy to apply at first, but once the connection was made, it held.

Keep in mind that to use eye contact and pausing skills effectively, you don't need to do anything out of the ordinary. Your eye contact during a presentation doesn't need to be more sustained than it is in informal conversation, and pauses don't need to be any longer. You just have to use these skills in the out-of-the-ordinary environment of presenting, so they may feel different to you. But they won't feel any different to your listeners. Another Winans insight that rings particularly true in this regard is that "it takes courage and self-control to speak straight to an audience."[4] We see this sort of courage and self-control put to the test in every workshop. To engage people in conversation is to open yourself up to them and to everything that entails.

Making These Skills Work for You

Everyone reacts differently to the challenge of engaging listeners. In our workshops, we assess each presenter's response to the process and find the simplest way to help them through the funhouse. For most people, it's not enough to say, "Make this a conversation and just be natural," because being nervous or self-conscious is perfectly "natural." Instead, we focus on helping presenters find the skill that will help them initiate the conversation—even when they're stressed.

If you were participating in one of our workshops, there would come a time when we would have to make you nervous. Well, that's not exactly it. It's more like we ask you to go to the front of the room when we know that doing so is going to be uncomfortable. This

4. Winans, *Public Speaking*, 34.

doesn't involve anything beyond asking you to speak to the others in the class, but if you're like most people, it's enough to put you in the funhouse.

The exercise, the first to be video recorded in the workshop, is a self-introduction. When it's your turn, you go to the front of the room and talk about your work and job responsibilities. You have no slides to rely on, no table to stand behind, and the camera is running. If you're like most people, your discomfort doesn't last very long, but what's important is that we get to see it. We're able to see and hear your unique response to the funhouse and the disengagement it brings. From there, we experiment with different skills and techniques until we find your exit from the funhouse.

Let's turn the discussion over to Greg and take a look at how these concepts play out for our class participants.

The Engagement Exercise

As Dale mentioned, the point of this first exercise is to figure out what each presenter needs to do to initiate a conversation with the audience. While we know that eye contact and pausing are the key skills involved, the funhouse affects your natural ability to use those skills well. To reduce the amount of time you spend in the funhouse, we need to explore its effect on what you do, think, and feel when you're in it.

To explain how this works, let's say you are participating in a workshop and I am sitting down with you to look at your first video. As we watch the video, my job is to guide you through the process. Our ultimate goal, along with sharpening your skills, is to build your self-awareness and objectivity so that you can be successful in a variety of situations.

As the video plays, I may ask you questions like these:

- Do you appear the way you thought you would when the video was shot?
- Are you surprised by what you see? If so, is it a good surprise or a not-so-good one?
- Do you remember seeing people's faces and responding to their reactions during the exercise?

Gestures, Stance, and Intonation

You might be wondering why we're not addressing traditional "delivery skills," such as gestures, stance, and intonation.

It's simple really. Addressing those things without talking about engagement is a hallmark of the performance approach.

- Are your pauses as long as they felt?
- When you paused like that, were you able to gather your thoughts and think? Did it give you the control you need to feel confident?
- Which skill, eye contact or pausing, is easier for you to focus on? Which one eases you into the conversation better?
- When you focus on a particular skill, does it have a secondary effect? If so, is that effect a good or bad thing?
- Once you're engaged, is there anything you're doing that's distracting to the audience? Were you aware of it at the time?

Your answers to questions like these help us understand more fully what your reaction to the funhouse actually is. After all, the funhouse is really nothing more than a state of mind that has a negative effect on your self-awareness and self-control. If we can figure out exactly what that negative effect is for you, we can address it.

Let's take a look at how this process worked for our presenters.

Michael faces very typical issues and provides a good example of how the process for getting engaged works.

During this exercise, Michael talked about his role at NHS and his responsibilities as a salesperson. When he was finished (and the camera was off), he described how it felt and received feedback from his peers and Dale. With the camera on again, Michael worked on improving his eye contact and pausing. After that, he talked about his experience and received more feedback from the group.

When this process was over, it was time to watch the video with me. Video in hand, the two of us walk down the hall. We enter a room. I close the door. We sit. "How'd it go?" I ask.

Responses to this question usually range from "terrible" to "that wasn't so bad." Michael said, "My mind was racing. It was similar to what I experience when I'm thrown off with my buyers. I have no idea what I said up there."

We hear that a lot, too. Not being entirely sure what just happened is a typical funhouse reaction.

Before we watch the video, I ask Michael how he wants to be perceived by his buyers. His answer to this question will help us stay focused. Michael said he'd like to be described as

- Honest
- On their side
- Helpful
- Trustworthy
- Not a used-car salesman

As we watch Michael's video, we'll keep these goals in mind. Does the person we see on video appear honest? On their side? Helpful? If his answer is yes, we will talk about why, and I'll reinforce whatever he's doing to make that impression. If his answer is no, it will focus our discussion on what it will take to make it to yes.

Michael said he didn't appear honest and trustworthy at first. He seemed unfocused, and what he said was unclear. He also said he spoke too much. "It was as if I ran out of things to say but just kept talking anyway. A person who knows what he's talking about wouldn't ramble like that."

Further, his eyes bounced around quite a bit and never quite landed on any one person for long. That became the focus as the exercise continued. Dale had him talk about a current business issue, this time extending his eye contact and making sure that he made a connection with each person. After watching that portion of the video, Michael said it looked better. When I asked him if he saw everyone's face, he said "yes." This is good. It's hard to hold a conversation with people when you're not seeing them.

"People in the class said I spoke too fast," Michael said. "I think they're right."

"Let's keep watching," I said. During

How long should I pause?

The challenge with pausing, especially for nervous presenters, is that it is absolutely uncomfortable. A moment's silence can feel like it stretches on forever.

Letting the silence happen, though, is a skill every presenter needs.

Keep in mind that when we say "pause," we're not talking about freezing the way you would during a game of freeze tag. Instead, think of it as "active pausing." During each active pause, you should be quite busy breathing, thinking ahead, and getting your thoughts together. Thankfully, it doesn't take much time for that to happen and that tiny pause reaps huge benefits.

Further, as counterintuitive as it seems, pausing makes you look confident and in control.

It's hard to hold a conversation with people when you're not seeing them.

the next section of the video, Michael was asked to focus on pausing between thoughts. Michael said he found it difficult to remember to pause, but when he did remember, he felt it gave him control over his racing mind. As he watched, he remarked how clear and focused he appeared. "I look like I know what I'm talking about!"

"You bet you do. And what's more is that your speaking pace is back to normal," I said. "You worked on eye contact and pausing. Based on what we see on the video, I think pausing is crucial for you. It gives you the control you need to gather your thoughts, and that helps you be clear."

"I agree," Michael said. "I just need to remember to do it."

I wrote on the flipchart: Michael—Pause to gather thoughts & slow down.

"Thanks," he said as he left to go back to the main classroom. "That wasn't so bad."

Pausing is the skill that helps Michael gain control and get engaged. We discovered that when he pauses just a little longer than feels necessary, he gives himself time to gather his thoughts. This, in turn, improves his self-awareness and helps him be clear and focused. It also brings his speaking pace under control.

Focusing on eye contact had some benefit for Michael, but pausing is what really gave him the control and presence of mind he needs to connect. Once he's connected, his eye contact improves naturally.

As we sat down, I asked, "How'd it go?"

"Not good," Terry replied. "But Jennifer said I looked great when I answered Dorothy's question."

"Let's take a look, but first, how would you like to be described by your audience members?"

Terry said he'd like to be described as

- Having executive presence
- Clear
- Concise
- In control

During the exercise, Terry had a hard time establishing eye contact with his audience. As he spoke, he scanned the room, looking *toward* the audience, but failing to make a connection with any single individual. His delivery was halting and difficult to watch. He held his arms awkwardly at his sides.

When I asked him what he was thinking about during this part of the video, he said, "I was in my head. I was thinking about how nervous I felt and what to do with my hands. I don't really remember what I said." In short, Terry had a funhouse reaction similar to Michael's.

Terry needed to direct his attention toward the audience. It was clear from the next section of video, that Dale had the same thought. To help Terry shift his focus outward, Dale had Dorothy ask him an easy-to-answer, job-related question. Terry's task was to answer the question while looking at Dorothy and not to worry about directing eye contact to anyone else in the room.

The result was a natural, comfortable, well-spoken answer. As Terry answered Dorothy's question, he stood tall, gestured naturally,

How long should eye contact be?

This question comes from people who have been taught from a performance perspective.

There is no perfect answer. It should be long enough to make a connection with the person. That will be different for everyone. If you're truly engaged, you'll know when it's time to move on. Here are some ideas people have found useful:

- **Keep your eye contact on a single person a little longer than feels necessary to you.**
- **Finish a thought while looking at one person, just as you do in regular conversation.**

You'll know your eye contact is good when you remember having seen people's faces as you spoke.

and looked comfortable. His focus was outward toward Dorothy, and he appeared engaged in the conversation. "That's better," he said, "I certainly look more in control."

"Does that guy have executive presence?" I asked.

"More than the first guy we saw," he said.

During that exercise, two things happened. First, we asked Terry to answer a question. Because he didn't know what the question would be, he didn't have the opportunity to worry about what he planned to say. Second, to ease Terry into the conversation, we had him focus his eye contact on just one person.

This is a simple exercise that took place in the controlled environment of the training room, but it's extremely useful. Through it, Terry was able to feel (and later see on video) what it's like to engage an audience member. That's the first step, to bring a single person into the conversation. Once a genuine connection is made with one person, it's much easier to bring others into the process. It just has to start somewhere.

Terry also experienced another surprise: he gestured freely without thinking about it. "What a relief not to have to hold my hands at my sides," he said. "I have been trying to follow that silly rule for years."

Unfortunately, Terry is not alone. We hear this sort of comment all the time. Because Terry has been following a rule about holding his hands at his sides, he was distracted, which in turn made speaking clearly even more difficult. Now that he understands that his first goal should be to get engaged (and that his hands will naturally know what to do when he does), he'll be in a better position to be clear and think on his feet. Even when things get heated.

Sophia

As we know, Sophia is an Entertainer. It's not unusual for someone like her to begin as if the stage lights have just come up. The good thing for Entertainers is that they are usually comfortable in front of people, and nervousness isn't an issue. Unfortunately, they usually have a rough time engaging people. The idea that a presentation is a controlled performance is so ingrained in them that knocking down the fourth wall, and speaking spontaneously, throws them off. This performance attitude needs to be unlearned.

What Sophia doesn't know is how high the stakes are. A few weeks before the workshop, Sophia's manager, Olive, called our office.

"I loved your class when I took it a few years ago," Olive began, "and I'm hoping you can help me with a situation with one of my direct reports. She is a wonderful, generous person. We're actually very good friends outside of work, which makes managing her a little tricky. Her name is Sophia, and I'm concerned about her credibility in the classroom. As my boss put it, Sophia wastes people's time and loses credibility when she leads training sessions. For example, earlier this week she had everyone do an icebreaker. These people have known each other for years. There was no ice to break! I've talked about this with her for some time now, but I don't think anything I've said has sunk in." Olive went on to say that she hoped we could help Sophia find a new approach. "Sophia doesn't know it, but my boss has given me an ultimatum. Sophia's job is on the line."

The insight I gained from that conversation was invaluable to me as Sophia's coach. The stakes, as it turns out, are high for both of us. I need to help Sophia keep her job.

Here's what we observed when we watched her video. Sophia walked to the front of the room and asked if the camera was on. Dale said, "Yes it's rolling, go ahead whenever you're ready." What happened next is a typical Entertainer moment. She turned on her smile and energetically introduced herself to the group. She lifted her right hand with great fanfare and held out three fingers as she said, "There are *three* things you should know about me." She proceeded to count them off as she continued. Her voice was singsong and her cadence was rhythmic, not at all like the Sophia we'd met earlier.

After a couple minutes, we hear Dale say, "Okay, Sophia, you're done. How'd that feel?"

Less energetically and with a sigh of relief, she said, "Good. I think I said everything that I planned to say."

We usually keep the camera rolling when Entertainers think it's off. Our goal is to capture them speaking naturally. We watched as Sophia listened to some feedback from the group and responded to them in her regular, non-presenter-mode voice.

Sophia giggled as she watched this and looked to me for reassurance.

Leaving the camera on, as sneaky as it seems, is very helpful during video review because the difference between the Entertainer on stage and the real person is stark. We're hoping that the Entertainer will see this contrast and acknowledge that entertaining is not the best approach. This recognition started to hit home with Sophia. She had said earlier that she'd like to be perceived as "genuine." As we watched her video, it became clear to her that she didn't seem genuine at all. "I'm sort of talking *at* them," she said. At that point, we were able to figure out together how she can settle into the conversation. She decided to focus on eye contact because it reminds her she's talking with real live people.

A secondary issue for Sophia is that she's naturally energetic, which can lead to a fast speaking pace. Pausing will help, but we'll take it one step at a time. The larger, more pressing issue is letting go of her performance approach.

Here's How the Others Did

Now let's see how the engagement exercise played out for the rest of the class participants.

People like Jennifer, our Nervous Perfectionist, often struggle with this exercise. They place the bar so high that it's unattainable. When asked how nervous they are, they usually respond with, "off the charts" or having had an "out-of-body experience." Like everyone else, Nervous Perfectionists need to find ways to settle into the conversation and be themselves. For Jennifer, it will start with pausing to breathe and settle her mind. Once she takes control of her thoughts, she'll feel more comfortable and confident.

She'll also be able to control her body. When we reviewed her video, she remarked how "crazed" she looked "pacing back and forth like that. I had no idea I did that."

"All that unnecessary movement is caused by your nervousness," I told her. "You were in the funhouse. Once you're engaged, your nervousness will decrease, and your self-awareness will increase. When that happens, you'll recognize that you're moving too much. Keep in mind that it's okay to move—you just need to do so with purpose."

How can I eliminate "ums?"

"You said seven 'ums' just now," Terry said to Jennifer.

Some people are overly concerned about filler words. Terry, our Dutiful Student, is one of them.

While filler words can sometimes be annoying, we've found that um, uh, like, and so on usually decrease when presenters are engaged. So rather than worrying about the occasional um or uh, we always recommend that presenters get comfortable with pausing first. The self-awareness gained through engagement usually results in fewer fillers.

Pausing will also help Luis. He doesn't suffer from nerves, but his thoughts are racing and muddled. Pausing will give him the time he needs to think and take control. This will help him project confidence. During the morning's goal-setting session, Luis said he wanted to project a professional image. Pausing will be the first step toward achieving that goal as well.

James lacks self-awareness and is a bit of a bulldozer. He doesn't mean to be, but his natural approach is to say what he wants to say regardless of how it is heard. People like James often say that they have very good eye contact, but when we watch the video, we see someone looking *through* people. He's looking in the general direction of his audience, but he fails to connect. When we get James to recognize the need for real eye contact and connection, he's more likely to read his audiences and respond to them appropriately.

Often in our workshops, we see people who are already good at engaging their listeners and don't experience any level of nervousness. James *thinks* he's in this group, but he's not.

Dorothy and Elaine had a fairly easy time with this exercise. They are both good at engaging their listeners. Most of our work with them will focus on message development and delivery. That's not to say eye contact and pausing aren't important for them. During the coaching session, Dorothy said she thought pausing would help her take more control over her presentations. Elaine said she thought pausing would help her avoid knee-jerk reactions when her presentations get heated.

Engagement Skills to Focus On

Michael
- Pause to gather thoughts + slow down

Terry
- eye contact to make a connection

Sophia
- eye contact; have a conversation with them

Jennifer
- Pause to breathe + think. Be aware of and control movement

Luis
- Pause to collect thoughts

James
- Eye contact; really see them, respond

Dorothy
- Pause to take control

Elaine
- Pause to avoid knee-jerk reactions

So What Does This Mean for You?

Nothing is more important than getting engaged and becoming self-aware. Once that happens, you may still have polishing to do, but that will be much easier once you're engaged in the conversation.

Contents

Chapter 7
Adapt to Your Default Approach

In this chapter . . .

- **Backstory**
- **What's Your Default Approach?**
- **A Look at the Assessment Results**
- **So What Does This Mean for You?**

Presentations succeed because they combine the focus and order of writing and the interactive spontaneity of conversation. Your reaction to the tension between the two is important. Before we discuss Defaults any further, we'd like you to complete the Default assessment on the following page. When you're finished, add up the number of statements you have marked in Column A and Column B. We'll come back to your results later.

With each pair of statements, choose the one that describes you better. Try not to answer them in terms of how you would like to see yourself, but in terms of how you actually are, or have tended to be in the past.

	A	B	
I feel that if I put a lot of work into my slides, I'll succeed.	O	O	I feel that slides are just a part of an effective presentation.
Organizing information comes easily to me.	O	O	Speaking to groups comes easily to me.
Whether it's true or not, I feel I'm more likely to succeed if I practice my presentation.	O	O	Whether it's true or not, I feel that I can wing it and be okay.
If I could, I'd deliver my presentation, then answer questions about it.	O	O	If I could make them that way, my presentations would be nothing but a series of questions and answers.
Having to make last-minute adjustments to my presentation frustrates me.	O	O	One of my fears is delivering my presentation and getting no response from my audience.
I like preparing more than presenting.	O	O	I like presenting more than preparing.
For me to feel confident, my presentation needs to take a logical path from A to B to C.	O	O	For me, a successful presentation could follow any path.
I spend a lot of time making sure my presentations are thorough and accurate.	O	O	Even when I have plenty of time to prepare, I often delay preparation until the last minute.
I feel confident that my presentations are well organized.	O	O	I feel confident that I can engage my audience in the conversation.
When I'm delivering a presentation, I often get too wrapped up in the details of my slides and forget about my audience.	O	O	When I'm delivering a presentation, I often lose track of or get ahead of my slides.
I feel that I am naturally organized.	O	O	I feel that I am naturally disorganized.
Timing the presentation exactly is part of being well prepared.	O	O	I tend to run out of time.
I find it difficult to speak off the cuff.	O	O	Speaking off the cuff is easy for me.

Backstory

Several years ago, I was working with a woman named Laura, a senior writer at a big corporation. When we discussed her goals at the beginning of class, she said she was very comfortable with the written word and loved the process of putting ideas on the page, but she absolutely dreaded her presentations. Presenting made her feel out of control, disorganized, and clumsy. She felt she never connected with her audience. "I'm at a point now," she said, "where I simply can't avoid presenting any longer."

I had seen this preference for the written word before, of course. It's common to hear people say that they would rather just write things down than talk about them, and vice versa. The interesting thing about Laura was the intensity of her reaction to presenting—and the accuracy of her personal insight. During the workshop, she was nervous, frustrated, and, as she said, unable to connect.

As I continued to work with her, I realized that her strengths as a writer were fiercely working against her ability to present. She had to resolve that conflict in order to improve her presentations. That meant making changes that, at least at first, felt very uncomfortable. For one thing, she needed to stop scripting herself—an idea she hated.

As class went on and Laura saw herself on video, she realized that she could be clear and persuasive when speaking off the cuff. She just had to get used to the idea that what *felt* uncomfortable to her *looked* very good. She realized that even though presenting might never be as natural to her as writing, she could still succeed.

After working with Laura, we started paying more attention to how presenters *feel* before and during their presentations. This isn't as strange as it sounds. We just ask which parts of the process feel easy and natural and which parts don't. We dig beneath the surface of nervousness and ask not only, "Do you get nervous when presenting?" but also, "What do you worry about when you're nervous?" and "Why do you worry about that?" We also ask presenters how they feel about preparation: "How much preparation do you need to feel confident?" And so on. From the responses we've received, we've learned three important things.

1. What presenters feel is deeply ingrained, and it is influenced by an enormous range of experiences. Your current job, past jobs, and what you studied in school are just the beginning. Some people carry the weight of a childhood public speaking experience well into adulthood.
2. These feelings have tremendous influence. They are the gauge you use at every stage of the process to measure your success—sometimes accurately, sometimes not.
3. Finally, and most important for this discussion, we learned that presenters could be classified into two distinct groups. Some favor the orderly side of presenting, and some favor the conversation side.

We decided to call these two classifications Default Approaches, because they describe your natural starting point—all the feelings, assumptions, and habits you bring to the process. Naming the approaches gave us a way to explain why one person might walk away from the workshop with a completely different set of recommendations than someone else. And why a one-size-fits-all approach actually fits no one.

Your Default is a result of the tension between order and the conversation. Improvement begins by accepting this tension and managing your response to it. If you are like most presenters, understanding your Default will bring a sense of relief. It identifies the struggle you face, validates what you feel, and points the way to improvement. Just as important, it helps you anticipate your knee-jerk reactions to the pressures of a demanding audience or nervous anxiety.

What's Your Default Approach?

The Default assessment you completed is not meant to be a scientific survey. It's simply a snapshot of your preferences. If you chose more items in Column A, you place a great deal of faith in preparation and default to an approach that prefers a controlled communication environment. We call people like you Writers. If you marked more statements in Column B, you believe in your ability to connect and respond to the audience. You are an Improviser.

Within each of these two basic Default Approaches, there are endless variations. If you're like most people, you are somewhere between the two extremes. Think of your score as the starting point for a more detailed look at how you work as a presenter. Also, keep in mind that Defaults are gut responses, not thoughtful choices. While everyone understands that presenters need to be prepared and initiate a conversation, individuals respond differently to the challenge. Here's what I mean.

Writers

If you're a Writer—that is, you checked more items in Column A—you're drawn to and are comfortable with the preparation process. The preparation you go through may take many forms—research, slide creation, outlining, scripting. Your allegiance to it could be a result of your comfort with the written word (like Laura) or data (technical and financial people, for example). Writers are sticklers for detail and predictability.

The benefit of being a Writer is that you're comfortable with the work that needs to be done before a presentation starts. The drawback is that you may assume preparation alone will guarantee success. If this were true, delivering the presentation would be just like sending an e-mail to every member of your audience. For many Writers, the energy spent creating slides, notes, and outlines is used to avoid thinking about actually delivering the presentation. When allowed to go unchecked, the Writer's approach can lead to

- Overreliance on the products of preparation—slides, notes, or scripts
- Failure to adapt to the immediate needs of the audience
- Frustration when listeners fail to understand or accept information immediately
- Frustration when questions are asked or comments are made
- The assumption that the slides speak for themselves
- Paralysis in the face of last-minute changes to the presentation's purpose, length, or audience
- A sense of success based on whether you said things the way you planned to say them

Writers need to remember that presenting is a process, not a product.

Writers need to remember that presenting is a process, not a product. While it's important to have a plan and do your best to follow it, presentations must be delivered in response to an audience. If you're a Writer, you need to trust yourself to deliver a clear, prepared message within the context of the conversation taking place. When you do, you will be spontaneous, flexible and organized.

Improvisers

When Improvisers are faced with the demands of presenting, they focus on the moment of delivery. If you're an Improviser—you have more checks in Column B—your sense of success lies in your ability to establish a connection with listeners. Improvisers struggle with preparation and often are unsure of how to get started. You may delay the preparation process, or maybe you second-guess at every turn, always toying with alternatives. You assume that what happens before the presentation is secondary to what happens during it. An Improviser's sense of comfort and control has to do with responding to a live audience.

The benefit of being an Improviser is that you're comfortable thinking on your feet, and you are, at least at first, easy to listen to. The drawback is that you often rely too heavily on your ability to seize the moment. Here are typical consequences of the Improviser's approach:

- Structure of the presentation is not clear.
- Delivery wanders and is difficult to follow.
- Slides are hastily put together and look it.
- Slides are ignored during delivery.
- What's on the screen does not reflect what's being said.
- Presenter feels successful simply because the presentation includes lively interaction.

Improvisers need to remember that listeners need help.

Improvisers need to remember that listeners need help. While Improvisers are comfortable with the notion that presentations are an unpredictable process, they need to remember that the process itself has to take place within an easily discernible structure. It is your responsibility to make the work of listening easier. Improvisers need to accept the idea that a well-prepared presentation is not a straightjacket. It's a framework strong enough to hold up the conversation.

Who are you more like?

Writers

- Focus goes to the plan
- Feel there is never enough time to prepare
- Need structure and predictability
- Are naturally thorough, careful, detailed, and accurate

Thrive with organization and preparation. But can be inflexible and strict during delivery.

Improvisers

- Focus goes to the people
- Delay preparation until the last minute
- Need to be spontaneous and engaged
- Are responsive and unafraid to make last-minute changes

Thrive with connection to listeners. But can lose focus and confuse listeners during delivery.

A Look at the Assessment Results

As class participants finish up their Default Assessment, I make a chart. The class is evenly split: four Writers and four Improvisers.

I always enjoy the discussions that take place when we talk about Defaults with class participants. As they begin to dig into the concept, we can see the light bulbs going on over their heads. They smile and nod, and a few eyes may widen in a how-did-you-know-that-about-me way. It's a little like reading your horoscope or a description of your Myers-Briggs personality type. You almost can't believe the truths you're reading about yourself.

More than that, I think the concept finally puts words to the struggles people have faced throughout their careers. Everyone knows that a presentation should feel conversational. The struggle is in how to make it that way. Understanding your Default helps you understand your path forward and the tools and techniques that will work for you (and the ones that won't).

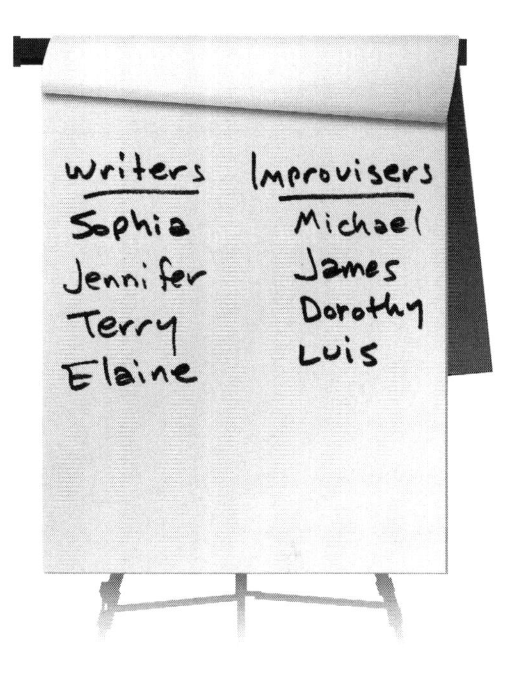

Since you've gotten to know the participants, you probably could have guessed at least some of their Default approaches. For example, it's clear from their comments early on and the work they did during the engagement exercise that Jennifer, the Nervous Perfectionist, and Terry, the IT-guy-turned-leader, are Writers. They both want their presentations to be predictable, and they worry a great deal about delivery. Jennifer checked every box in the Writer column on her assessment.

We could also have guessed that Michael, the sales guy, and James, the packaging business owner, are Improvisers given their desire for a two-way conversation. While James's assessment wasn't quite as lopsided as Jennifer's, it's still fairly clear where he falls.

JAMES

	A	B	
I feel that if I put a lot of work into my slides, I'll succeed.	○	✓	I feel that slides are just a part of an effective presentation.
Organizing information comes easily to me.	○	✓	Speaking to groups comes easily to me.
Whether it's true or not, I feel I'm more likely to succeed if I practice my presentation.	○	✓	Whether it's true or not, I feel that I can wing it and be okay.
If I could, I'd deliver my presentation, then answer questions about it.	✓	○	If I could make them that way, my presentations would be nothing but a series of questions and answers.
Having to make last-minute adjustments to my presentation frustrates me.	✓	○	One of my fears is delivering my presentation and getting no response from my audience.
I like preparing more than presenting.	○	✓	I like presenting more than preparing.
For me to feel confident, my presentation needs to take a logical path from A to B to C.	○	✓	For me, a successful presentation could follow any path.
I spend a lot of time making sure my presentations are thorough and accurate.	○	✓	Even when I have plenty of time to prepare, I often delay preparation until the last minute.
I feel confident that my presentations are well organized.	○	✓	I feel confident that I can engage my audience in the conversation.
When I'm delivering a presentation, I often get too wrapped up in the details of my slides and forget about my audience.	✓	○	When I'm delivering a presentation, I often lose track of or get ahead of my slides.
I feel that I am naturally organized.	✓	○	I feel that I am naturally disorganized.
Timing the presentation exactly is part of being well prepared.	○	✓	I tend to run out of time.
I find it difficult to speak off the cuff.	○	✓	Speaking off the cuff is easy for me.

An interesting thing about James's assessment is that he *feels* organized, which goes against the feedback he's received from his coworker. They both can't be right, so like a lot of other people, James might feel one way but actually *be* another.

Presenters need to accept that sometimes what they feel is inaccurate. Because James feels organized, he may never have done anything to ensure that he actually was organized. As a result, he has frustrated and confused his audiences and coworkers. The first step for James is to put more thought into preparing than he feels he needs to.

As Dale mentioned, the idea that everyone has a Default Approach was the result of our efforts to figure out what individual presenters needed to do to improve. We had known for years that a one-size-fits-all approach didn't work. By identifying a presenter's Default, we found a way to explain why.

I remember working with an MBA named Brian a few years ago. He was a Marketing Manager at a big beverage company. He regularly delivered presentations to his boss and the brand management team, and they were an unruly bunch. On a good day, a presentation to this group ended in a lively discussion. On a bad day, the meetings were free-for-alls. Brian was okay with this. When he had a presentation to prepare, he collected his data, put it in the same order as always, and that was about it.

Then Brian got a new boss. After the first presentation he heard Brian deliver, the boss said, "Brian, you had a lot of good data there, but do everyone a favor next time and put together an agenda. Your presentation was all over the place." Although he didn't say it, Brian thought his boss was wrong. "There is no way," he thought, "this group is going to pay any attention to an agenda."

Brian did what his boss asked. For his next presentation, he put together a very simple agenda and brought it up on the screen as he began, "Okay, everyone, here's the agenda I'd like to go through today." To his surprise, it worked. The brand management team didn't chuckle and actually seemed to appreciate that Brian's presentation had some sort of structure. They still interrupted, of course, and occasionally went off track. But as loose as its organization was, the presentation was efficient and business got done.

Brian didn't have the words for it at the time, but he's an Improviser. By creating a simple agenda and allowing the conversation to take place within its framework, he was able to deliver his message clearly and efficiently while also being responsive. This discovery helped Brian change his approach and trust his boss.

Getting back to our class, let's look at Sophia. Unlike Brian, she has not been very responsive to her boss's feedback. Despite Olive's attempts to steer her in a different direction, Sophia feels that her performance approach *should* be right, so she sticks with it. On the surface this looks like stubbornness. If we dig a little deeper, though, we can see that Sophia simply has the wrong goal in mind. She wants her training sessions to be enjoyable when her goal should be to create the conditions for fruitful learning.

If we go back to what Sophia said during the goals discussion, you'll remember she said, "I think the key to success is being prepared. I practice a lot before each training session I lead." That sounds like something a Writer would say. On the other hand, she checked the box for "Speaking to groups comes easily to me" on her assessment. These two statements seem to be in conflict.

Let's look at Sophia's assessment in more detail As you can see, she checked more boxes on the left than the right, which means she leans more toward the Writer side. She does, though, have some Improviser traits.

Sophia

	A	B	
I feel that if I put a lot of work into my slides, I'll succeed.	●	○	I feel that slides are just a part of an effective presentation.
Organizing information comes easily to me.	○	●	Speaking to groups comes easily to me.
Whether it's true or not, I feel I'm more likely to succeed if I practice my presentation.	●	○	Whether it's true or not, I feel that I can wing it and be okay.
If I could, I'd deliver my presentation, then answer questions about it.	●	○	If I could make them that way, my presentations would be nothing but a series of questions and answers.
Having to make last-minute adjustments to my presentation frustrates me.	○	●	One of my fears is delivering my presentation and getting no response from my audience.
I like preparing more than presenting.	○	●	I like presenting more than preparing.
For me to feel confident, my presentation needs to take a logical path from A to B to C.	●	○	For me, a successful presentation could follow any path.
I spend a lot of time making sure my presentations are thorough and accurate.	●	○	Even when I have plenty of time to prepare, I often delay preparation until the last minute.
I feel confident that my presentations are well organized.	○	●	I feel confident that I can engage my audience in the conversation.
When I'm delivering a presentation, I often get too wrapped up in the details of my slides and forget about my audience.	●	○	When I'm delivering a presentation, I often lose track of or get ahead of my slides.
I feel that I am naturally organized.	●	○	I feel that I am naturally disorganized.
Timing the presentation exactly is part of being well prepared.	●	○	I tend to run out of time.
I find it difficult to speak off the cuff.	○	●	Speaking off the cuff is easy for me.

The items she checked on the right—the Improviser side—are interesting because they all involve her perception of having a high comfort level with group interaction. If we look at everything she's said thus far in the class, my conversation with her manager, and the results of her Default Assessment, two things come into focus:

1. She sees value in the rich results of a lively conversation in the training room, but she's torn between that understanding and her desire to control the conversation.
2. To deal with this tension, she's manipulated the conversation inorganically. She's done this by using icebreakers, recreating what she's rehearsed, and relying on performance techniques.

Sophia has the potential to be an excellent presenter and trainer, but she needs to give up some of the control she exercises over the process. She needs to lay the groundwork for a rich and relevant conversation that members of her audience will want to participate in. That requires a shift in her thinking and a different set of skills and techniques than she's currently using. We made progress during our previous coaching session. Hopefully, we'll be able to continue along that path.

So What Does This Mean for You?

For starters, it's important to reserve judgment. Neither Default is better or more efficient. While it might be easy to assume that Improvisers are naturally more effective, it's not the case. Both Defaults have strengths and weaknesses. As the "Who Are You More Like?" graphic (page 90) shows, Writers thrive with organization and preparation but can be inflexible and strict during delivery. Improvisers, on the other hand, thrive with their connection

Both Writers and Improvisers improve by moving toward the opposite Default.

to listeners but can lose focus and cause confusion during delivery. Both Writers and Improvisers improve by moving toward the opposite Default.

In general terms,

- Writers need to let go of the control they want to exert over the process and trust themselves to speak spontaneously.
- Improvisers need to rein things in and build in structure so that what they say has context and makes sense to others.

So far we've talked about redefining business presentations, abandoning a performance approach in favor of engaging your listeners, and your Default response to the tension between order and conversation. Next we'll focus on the best way to prepare for an Orderly Conversation.

Contents

Chapter 8
Prepare to Be Flexible

In this chapter . . .

- **The Presentations**
- **What Their Success Will Look Like**
- **Getting Started**
- **The Planning Process**
- **Some Comments from the Presenters**
- **So What Does This Mean for You?**

Greg:

We've talked about the Orderly Conversation as a unique form of communication, how you react to the tensions it involves, and how to engage your listeners. In this chapter we'll focus on preparation, the work you do in advance to bring order and flexibility to the conversation. As we know from Chapter 2, presentations succeed on two levels.

- **Reaching your objective** Does the audience do what you want them to do, or understand what you want them to understand?
- **Managing the process** Do you initiate and manage a satisfactory interaction with your audience?

Planning needs to focus on both levels, but in many ways, the second is more important. There are a couple reasons for this.

First, as you know, business rarely gets done in a linear fashion. It is often one step forward and two steps back or one step forward and then another to the side. Because of this, it's not always possible to meet your objectives with every person in the audience every time you present. What you can work toward, though, is progress—a step in the right direction.

Second, keep in mind that business audiences are captive groups. They cannot walk out on a bad presentation, but they can disengage from it. They might feel a sudden need to text someone, check their e-mail, or simply start thinking about something else. Most of the time, this reaction has little to do with the objective of the presentation and everything to do with whether the presenter is managing the conversation effectively. Achieving your objective requires keeping the audience with you.

By achieving your second goal, then, you earn the audience's trust. We don't mean trusting that you are an honest person or one who can be depended upon, although these things are important. The audience members will trust you to make the work they are there to do no more difficult or time-consuming than it needs to be. When you earn that type of trust, your audience will feel that you are up to the task and will be more willing to get down to work.

Let's look at the presentation environment each of the workshop participants is facing.

The Presentations

We asked each of our presenters to bring in a presentation they have coming up. Here's how they described their audiences, their presentation goals, and the challenges they expect.

Terry

Terry: State of the Unit

I'm working on what we call the State of the Unit presentation. All the different business units present to the executive leadership team and their direct reports. These presentations tend to be rather formal and are sort of a tradition at BakleTech. It's a year-end presentation that focuses on our accomplishments over the past 12 months, our goals for the upcoming year, and the challenges we think we'll have. Preliminary budgets will also be included.

The VP of Sales will be there, of course, and that freaks me out. My slides will eventually be put into a template they give us.

Dorothy: Market Research

I'm working on this month's market research meeting. This is the one I have to deliver to the sales force in my region. They're a wiggly bunch, and I have got to get a handle on dealing with them. They don't report to me, so it's hard to make them pay attention. The content is organized the same every month. I'll talk about the market data collected since our last meeting, the sales promotions and results, and the competitor analysis. I'll wrap it up with the trends we're seeing in the market.

I just saw an e-mail that there was a fire in Sedgwick, and the roofing may be to blame for fueling the fire. I don't think it was our product on the building, but we sell to stores in that area, and I'm guessing we'll have to deal with some questions. It's not uncommon for a fire or other tragedy to spark media frenzy about raw materials and the safety of products in the construction industry. I think I should add this to my presentation.

Michael: One-to-One Sales Call

The presentation I'm working on is about a promotion NHS is rolling out. It's called Healthy Holiday. It's a follow-up to a really successful promotion we just completed, called Healthy Summer. Healthy Holiday is focused on people who want to stay healthy during the time of year when it's really difficult to eat right. This consumer is already pretty health conscious. They're runners, swimmers, bike riders—people who try to take care of themselves.

My goal is to get Colleen, the buyer at Super-Market—this is the person I mentioned earlier with the gymnast daughters—to agree to the promotion. It involves coupons in the circular and an in-store hutch display (one of those stand-alone racks) to create in-store excitement. The promotion will run in November and December.

I pulled a few slides together, but I really don't have enough information yet to flesh them out. The numbers won't be ready from the people in Sales Planning for another week or so.

Jennifer: A New Reimbursement Process

This is the presentation I mentioned earlier about the new reimbursement process. I like the process, so I'm comfortable with the content. The slides are pretty much ready to go. I just have a few more adjustments to make.

I'll be delivering it to the accounting department first. They all know about the new process, so my presentation to them will be mostly for us to confirm that we're all on the same page. They will give me feedback on the presentation and then I'll deliver it several times to groups of admins, IT, HR, and all the other areas of the firm. I won't be delivering it to any of the attorneys, though, and I'm really happy about that. My manager will handle them.

James: Sales Presentation

This is a sales presentation to one of our really big prospects. Kim, the new VP of Sales, thinks the timing is right for us to close the deal. So, she's asked me to join the meeting. As I said earlier, I'm there to be the figurehead.

On our side of the table, there will be three of us—Kim, John the

Account Manager, and me. Kim is there to close the deal. John will be the client's primary contact moving forward, so he's there to get the buyer comfortable with him. I'm there to provide a little context and, frankly, to make the buyer feel important.

I'll use those slides that Kim put together for me.

Sophia: Training Initiative

The presentation I'm working on? It's part of a training initiative at the credit union. We're rolling it out in a couple months. The instructional design and slides are pretty much ready to go. It's for our Member Service Reps (MSRs) and Account Managers. The class is called "Member Service 2.0," and it's designed to help our MSRs sell some of the add-on services we offer to our members.

Well, maybe *sell* is too strong a word. I think what we're trying to do is to identify opportunities by getting the MSRs listening and probing better when they talk to our members. If a member seems like a good candidate for an add-on, that information would be passed on to an Account Manager who would follow up on it.

The problem is that some of the MSRs are a little reluctant, shall we say. Especially those two I mentioned earlier. They feel that it's not their job to sell anything. Some of them have long-standing relationships with our members and feel those relationships will be compromised if they start upselling. That's their word, not mine. I see their concern, but the MSRs are our primary contact with clients. They might talk to them every few weeks. We're just trying to take advantage of that.

So really, the training is designed to do two things. First, get the MSRs to buy into this whole idea of Member Service 2.0. Second, give them the knowledge and skills they need to bring the add-ons into the conversations they have with clients. They'll need to change their approach a little, but I know they can do it.

Luis: Venture Capital

My team is presenting to some executives at a venture capital firm. Several of them will be in the room. Our goal is to impress them so that they'll invest in us; we need funding in order to grow the business. There will probably be about 10 other start-ups presenting that day, all competing for the same pot of money, so the competition is tough and the stakes are high. I'm the main presenter. The CTO will be there to address technology-specific questions, and I want our CMO to be there to talk about our go-to-market strategy if it comes up.

I'm told that VCs are impatient, and I have only a few minutes to make them trust me.

Elaine: Town Meeting

I'm not sure specifically which community people will be in the audience. It depends on several factors. But there are usually people on my side and people on the opposing side. The Egelton town council will be there too. This particular council tends to be pro-business, and we'll be bringing plenty of economic activity to the area during construction, so I think they'll be an easy audience. It's the people in the neighborhood I am concerned about.

My goal is to convince them that rezoning the block across from the library, which will give us the freedom to tear down the existing building and build a pedestrian-friendly mixed-use residential and retail structure, will be good for the community. The building and parking lot that's there used to be a national book retailer. It's been sitting empty for nearly three years. It's an eyesore, and you'd think they'd want it to be fixed up. I understand, though, that they opposed the building construction in the first place. Apparently, before the book retailer built its store, the land was a dog park.

What Their Success Will Look Like

Each of our presenters has a specific goal and clear insight into their audience. In the next section, we'll help them prepare for their presentations. Our goal will be, as Dale said earlier, to help them succeed on two levels. Here's what that means for the presenters.

Terry wants to convince the execs that his funding request should go through. He also wants to improve the impression he made on them during a previous presentation by establishing himself as a good communicator and leader. This can happen regardless of the funding decision.

When Dorothy, Jennifer, and Sophia deliver their presentations, their audiences want easy-to-understand information, delivered concisely, from a trusted source. All three need to focus on what the audience needs, and not overload them with unnecessary detail.

Michael needs to keep Colleen's trust even if she refuses the recommendations he's making today. He wants her to see him as someone she can do business with. The same is true for James. As the figurehead at the meeting, he needs to represent Jones & Harvey appropriately.

Elaine and Luis need to be clear, confident, and concise. They also need to earn the trust of a skeptical group of strangers very quickly.

Let's talk now about getting started.

Getting Started

For each of our presenters, traditional speechwriting strategies would fall short. The most familiar of these is the tell-them strategy. ("Tell them what you're going to tell them. Tell them. Tell them what you told them.") This approach frames a speech in a good way, but because it assumes that the process is only about *telling*, it isn't enough for a business presentation. Another popular approach, beginning with a shocking statistic or attention grabber, is usually too heavy-handed for presenters. These techniques might work at a shareholder meeting or to rally the troops, but not when the goal of the meeting is to hold a fruitful conversation.

During the first few minutes of your presentation, your job is to assure the audience members that you are not going to waste their time and attention. You do so by answering these questions from their point of view.

- Why are we here, and what do we need to accomplish?
- How will you get us there?
- How is this relevant and beneficial to us?

During the first few minutes of your presentation, your job is to assure the audience members that you are not going to waste their time and attention.

Answering these questions gives listeners a sense of purpose, a sense of direction, and a reason to participate. This frames the presentation in the audience's context and eliminates any confusion about what is to come. This seems like an easy thing to do, but it's usually not. Even the most experienced presenters have to work hard to pull themselves out of their own perspective—their own way of looking at things, even their own level of knowledge—to build this frame.

Part of this process is thinking about the larger conversation your presentation takes place within. Here are some examples:

- Terry's presentation is part of an annual meeting involving a series of presentations, so he'll need to pay close attention to what comes before him.
- Dorothy knows she needs to say something about the fire in Sedgwick.
- The context for Elaine's presentation may be influenced by a conversation she has with an Egelton resident as they both arrive for the meeting.

The context for your presentation might be the last meeting you had, the phone call from yesterday, or a question asked of a previous presenter. Placing your presentation in its context will make it feel like a natural extension of what came before. This will establish you as the person with perspective and the one who is in charge of this particular part of the larger conversation.

The presenters in our workshop use a handout to guide them through the planning process. If you'd like to use it, you can download a free copy at www.TheOrderlyConversation.com/tools. Here's how it works.

The Planning Process

We recommend "going analog" as you begin. By picking up a pen and paper and not opening up PowerPoint, you avoid the trap of worrying about slide design prematurely. This will help you gain the perspective you need to frame the conversation. The recommendation to go analog is also found in Nancy Duarte's *Slide:ology* and Garr Reynolds's *Presentation Zen*. In both books, the authors emphasize the need to take a step back from the details of your content and slides to focus on overall goals.[5]

---

5. Nancy Duarte, *Slide:ology: The Art and Science of Creating Great Presentations* (Sebastopol, CA: O'Reilly Books, 2008), 28–29.
   Garr Reynolds, *Presentation Zen: Simple Ideas on Presentation Design and Delivery* (Berkeley, CA: New Riders, 2008), 45–53.

Step One: Identify Your Goal

The first step is to identify what you want your audience to do, think, or feel at the end of the presentation. The best way to do this is to complete this sentence: At the end of my presentation, I want my audience to (do, think, or feel) _____. It's a good idea to limit yourself to a single sentence, because it forces you to be specific. In some situations, this will be an easy thing to do. In others, it won't. Here are some ideas to keep in mind.

- In **persuasive situations,** you're making a recommendation or asking your audience to do something. For example, Luis wants his audience to invest in 14 Ways. Elaine wants to convince everyone in her audience that it's a good idea to rezone the property her company wants to develop.
- With **informative presentations**, it's important to emphasize how you want your audience to think or feel about the information you're delivering. For example, if Jennifer simply said, "I want my audience to understand the new process," she's not focusing on what she wants them to think or feel. So instead of simply focusing on understanding, she could say, "I want my audience to *buy in* to the new process and *feel comfortable* using it."

It's important to articulate your objective clearly and carefully. The rest of your presentation will be built to achieve it.

Step Two: Assess Your Audience

Take a step back and think about the people in your audience. Consider questions like these:

- Who is your audience, and what is their relationship to you?
- Are there key people in your audience?

- What are your audience's pain points?
- Is the audience a cohesive group with similar needs? If not, how do they differ?
- What tensions exist within the group and the organization as a whole?

Also consider your audience's perspective on your topic and goal.

- How much do they understand about your topic?
- How much do they care about your goal? Is it important to them?
- Do some audience members understand or care about your topic more than others?
- Will they be difficult to persuade?

Whether it's natural for you or not, it's usually a good idea to be a little skeptical at this point. For example, imagine delivering your presentation when your audience is having a bad day. Think about a slightly exaggerated level of negativity or indifference from them. This will help you anticipate potential objections.

Step Three: Name Their Current Situation

After you've thought about your goal and your audience, think about what will be on your audience's mind at the beginning of your presentation. What is their current situation?

With persuasive presentations, the current situation usually reflects the opportunity, problem, or obstacle your presentation addresses:

- A retailer wants to increase sales or market share.
- A process isn't working, and it's frustrating everyone.
- A buyer is looking for the best product or service.

With informative presentations, the current situation recognizes that the group needs the information you're delivering.

- They need an update on the project you're working on.
- A new process has been put into place, and the audience needs to understand what it is.
- They need the information you have to make a decision.

The current situation often acknowledges the audience's state of mind:

- They're frustrated by a setback of some kind.
- They're uncomfortable with changes taking place.

As I said before, identifying the current situation at this stage in the process will help you focus on the context in which your presentation takes place. Demonstrating your awareness of that context will help you build trust.

Step Four: Organize Your Agenda

The agenda is simply a list of things you are going to talk about during the presentation. As you lay out your agenda, be sure to include everything your audience wants and needs to know to help you reach your goal. To make sure you don't waste anyone's time, omit information that's not relevant to the conversation.

Presenters rarely ask about how the body of their presentations should be laid out. Sometimes this is because the agenda follows a natural progression from A to B to C. In other situations, the audience asks that information be delivered in a certain way.

When you anticipate resistance from your audience, consider ordering the agenda to reflect their concerns, from most to least important. You will have a better chance of keeping listeners with you if you talk about their biggest concerns first.

Step Five: Identify Benefits to Your Audience

Think about what your audience will gain from your presentation. When you're delivering a persuasive presentation, think about how the audience benefits by taking your recommendation:

- Higher sales, greater profit, less waste
- Lower turnover, happier employees
- Satisfied customers

With a more informative presentation, think about the benefits of understanding:

- Informed enough to make a decision
- Clear up confusion
- Know how to function after reorganization

Step Six: Assign Action Steps

Identify the action(s) you want your audience members to take at the end of your presentation. Your action steps should be specific and fairly immediate.

Greg:

Some Comments from the Presenters

It's the afternoon of the first day of the workshop. All of our presenters are working through the handout Dale just summarized. Here are a couple of issues that surfaced for our group.

Assessing the Audience

Dorothy admitted somewhat sheepishly that she never bothers to think about these things ahead of time. She's not alone. In our experience, the idea of thinking about the audience and their wants and needs isn't new to people, but actually *doing it* is—especially when you're delivering information internally to people you know well. For every presentation, though, it's important to take the time to hone your message for that specific group of people at that particular moment in time.

Finding the Benefits for Informative Presentations

Sometimes the benefits of your presentation come simply from listening to or participating in the conversation. For example, in Dorothy's situation, the benefit for her audience of salespeople is that they will be able to take her information and repackage it for their sales pitches.

Jennifer said, "My presentation is purely informative. I'm not persuading them to fill out the reimbursement form. They don't have a choice in it. So, there's really no benefit for them, is there?" James jumped in and reminded her that the employees will get reimbursed more quickly, which is, of course, a benefit to them.

So What Does This Mean for You?

In this chapter, we went analog and began to build the foundation for each person's presentation. If you tracked along, perhaps working on your own presentation, you may have made some interesting discoveries. Here are some possibilities:

- You may have realized that the level of detail you thought you needed to go into isn't necessary, since you now understand that your audience already has a pretty good grasp of your topic.
- You may have discovered that your audience has some misconceptions and that you'll need to address those early on.
- You may have discovered that you need to rethink how persuasive you'll make the presentation.
- You might have recognized the need to acknowledge a negative current situation.
- Or, you might have realized that by naming the benefits, you'll gain buy-in sooner.

These discoveries are easier to make when you put pen to paper before opening up your presentation software.

Contents

Chapter 9
Create Framing Slides

In this chapter . . .

- **Traditional Thinking about Visual Aids**
- **Two Kinds of Slides: Framing and Content**
- **How to Get the Conversation Going**
- **Create Framing Slides for the Introduction**
- **Create a Framing Slide for the Conclusion**
- **So What Does This Mean for You?**

In this chapter, we focus on the visual component of your presentations. We didn't use the phrase "visual aids" to describe this part of the process, for reasons we examine next.

Traditional Thinking about Visual Aids

It's not that there's anything inherently wrong with calling your presentation materials visual aids, but the phrase is strongly associated with traditional speechmaking practices, many of which need to be reexamined in light of the Orderly Conversation. The most widely accepted of these practices is the notion that visual aids are, and should always be, subordinate to the speaker. During your presentations, that is not always the case.

Here are some other traditional assumptions about visual aids.

- Visual aids must be simple and communicate their message quickly.
- Graphics are better than words.

- Bullet points are boring.
- "Eye charts" (detailed slides with words and numbers too small for the audience to read) should never be used.

There is truth in each of these statements, but for business presenters they're only partial truths. They are not true all of the time or in every situation.

As you've probably seen in the business presentations you have been a part of, people bring a broad range of visual support to their presentations, much of it going far beyond the limits of traditional visual aids. Here are some examples of very common types of visual support.

- Reports that tell the audience how the business is doing
- Data that audience members will use in their own presentations to other audiences
- Maps, floor plans, photographs, drawings
- Forms audience members will have to fill out
- Demos of software and other processes

Much of this information is delivered using presentation software—PowerPoint or Keynote. (When referring to projected visuals, we'll call them "slides" unless there's reason to do otherwise.) But presenters also use flip charts, whiteboards, and video. In informal settings, presenters use tablets and other devices to display data. They often distribute handouts, brochures, sell sheets, or hard copies of the slides they're using. With the growth of webcasting and video, visuals are becoming even more complex. Among our workshop participants, we see even more options being used. Elaine plans to place posters around the room, each illustrating a different view of the development her company is proposing. Michael will take product samples to his sales meeting. All of these enrich the conversation.

Two Kinds of Slides: Framing and Content

The range of visual support you use can be divided by function into two fundamental categories: framing slides and content slides. Framing slides help you keep the conversation orderly. Content slides are the subject of the conversation.

- **Framing slides.** The slides that you use to introduce and conclude your presentation are framing slides. If you use recurring agenda slides in the body of the presentation, as we are doing in this book at the beginning of each chapter, they are also framing slides. The purpose of these slides is to give you a way to talk about the conversation itself, what it's about, why it's happening, how it's structured, and so on.

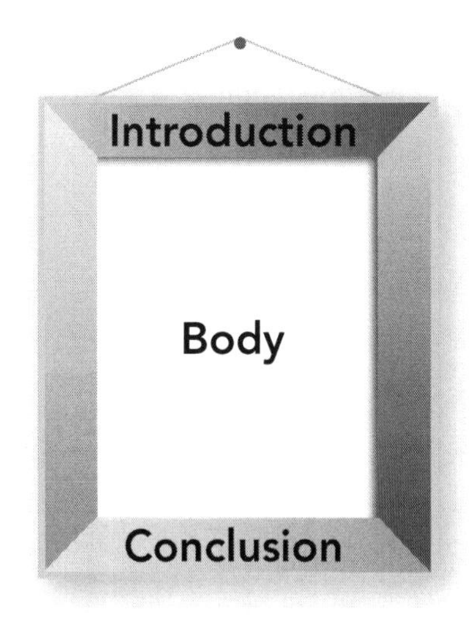

- **Content slides.** The visuals in the body of your presentation are content slides. They deliver the information and ideas that are the subject of the conversation. We'll talk more about content slides in Chapter 10.

Framing slides help you keep the conversation orderly. Content slides are the subject of the conversation.

For now, let's turn our attention to our presenters and watch as they work on framing their presentations.

How to Get the Conversation Going

When we ask workshop participants how we can help them prepare for their presentations, most people, like Terry and Sophia, ask about getting started. Terry said, "I mean, I'm fine putting together the details of what I need to say, but the beginning is always rough." Even after they've prepared good introductory slides, workshop participants still struggle as they talk through the opening of the presentation for the first time.

The reason for this is because they're preparing for a *conversation*. Figuring out how to start that conversation during the silence of preparation isn't easy. The goal for this part of the workshop is to help the presenters find the best way to do that.

As the presenters start to build the frame for their presentations, they'll stay analog, using stickies. Sticky notes are small. They force you to boil ideas down to the essentials.

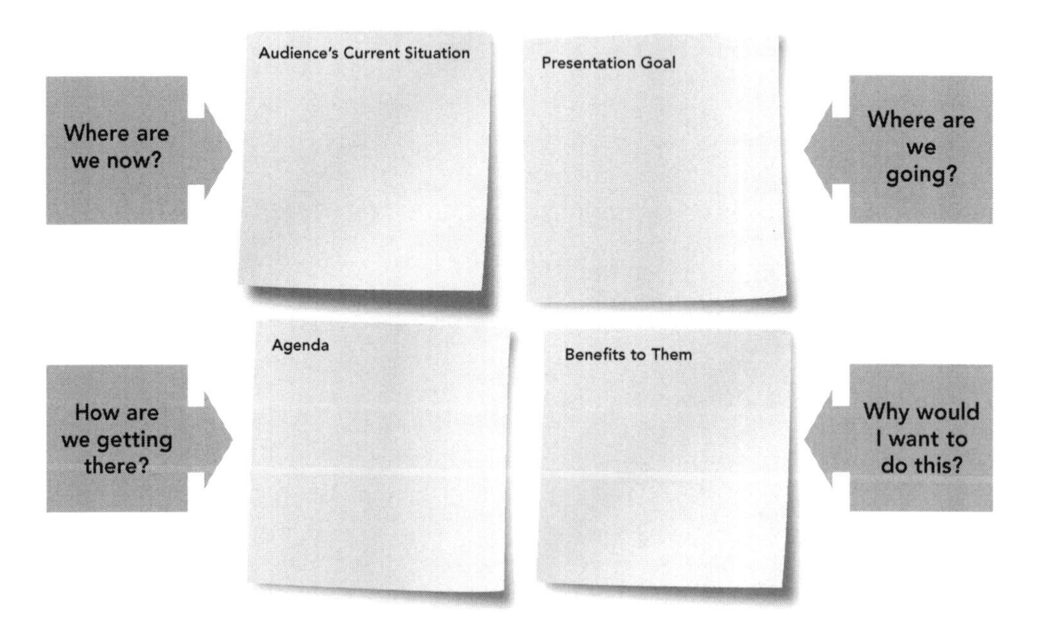

We ask everyone to lay out four stickies in this configuration. The labels should look familiar; they are taken from the handout we used earlier. As the arrows indicate, each sticky note answers an important question for your audience.

We have found this to be a useful starting point. You're able to see your main points in one place and tinker with the order very easily. Here's an example.

Let's say I'm a salesperson for Widgets USA, and my buyers sit at the corporate level and make company-wide decisions. Because we've experienced sluggish sales, one of my largest customers is considering eliminating our products from their stores nationwide. The goal of my presentation is to stop that from happening. Luckily, my R&D team is one step ahead of my customer. My stickies look like this.

Current situation:
Sluggish sales
Reconsidering relationship & carrying our products

Presentation goal:
RETHINK

Agenda:
· Research findings
· New product line
· Rollout schedule

Benefits:
Improved Sales
Happier customers

Create Framing Slides for the Introduction

By looking at the slides below, you can see how the ideas on my stickies became the introductory slides for my Widgets presentation. Let's look at some ways I can use them to frame the conversation.

Currently

- Sluggish sales
- Reconsidering relationship

Hi, everyone. As we all know, sales have been sluggish, and you're reconsidering our relationship and thinking about pulling Widgets USA products off your shelves.

Goal

- Rethink

My goal today is to ask you to rethink that.

Agenda

- Research findings
- New product line
- Rollout schedule

We conducted some research, and I want to show you our findings from that. I'll also talk about our new product line, and finally I'll go over a recommended rollout schedule.

Benefits

- Improved sales
- Happier consumer

When we're done, we'll have a clear path forward to improving sales and having happier consumers.

As you can see, I followed the same order as the stickies and gave my buyer a sense of direction, purpose, and a reason to participate in this conversation. I purposefully did not add any design elements to the slides, because I wanted to focus exclusively on the content. The next time through, I'll add design. I've also rearranged the order of the slides so that you can see how this framing strategy can be used in different ways. I'll begin with the benefits for a more positive start.

Hi, everyone. Today I'd like to talk about ways we're working to improve your sales.

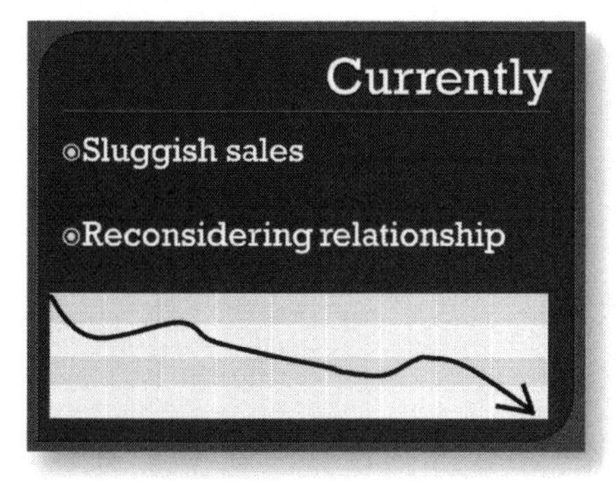

As we know, it's been a rough year. Sales have been sluggish, and as you shared with me last month, you're reconsidering our relationship.

Today, I'm asking you to rethink that.

To that end, I'll talk about three things. One: our research findings. Two: A whole new product line we developed as a result of the research. And Three: our recommended rollout schedule. Let's get going.

There you have two slightly different versions of my Widgets USA introduction. As you can see, the framing strategy is flexible, and the slides can be arranged in any order.

Make the Introduction Your Own

People often ask if it's okay to pull out one of the parts or combine multiple parts on one slide. Maybe there's some redundancy, or something simply feels uncomfortable. You might also have a specific reason for putting them in a different order. This is fine. The strategy is meant to be flexible and useful in a broad range of situations. Just keep the goals in mind. You're looking for a quick and easy way to give your listeners a sense of direction, purpose, and a reason to participate. How you get there is up to you.

Most people find great comfort in finally having a workable strategy for getting started, and this group was no exception. Let's take a look at a few of the approaches our participants used to frame their presentations. As you can see, everyone does a nice job.

Use Transitional Phrases: Terry. Here are Terry's stickies:

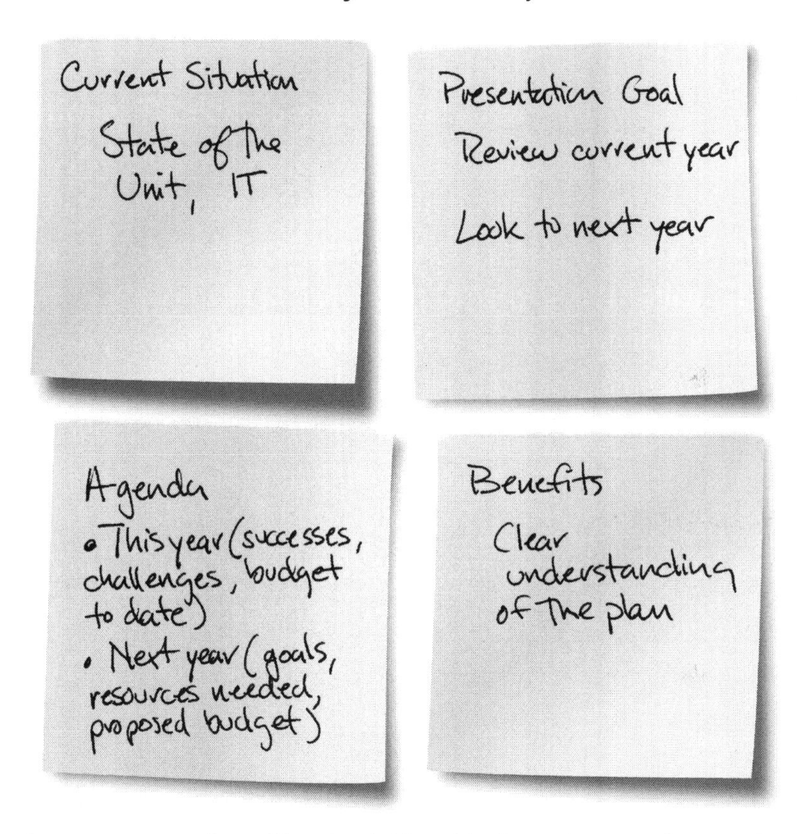

As you can see from Terry's stickies, his thoughts are clear and concise. Given the issues he brought into the class, this is a very big deal for him.

In addition, look at his agenda. He broke it down into two categories: this year and next year. Then he added some subordinate points to each. His agenda will communicate structure and make him appear organized.

Terry followed the introduction strategy without any changes; however, when he talked it through the first time, he had a hard time making it flow. He said he was searching for words and that the ideas didn't connect for him.

He needed to refer to how the slides fit into the context of the presentation. Here are some phrases that can help everything flow together easily.

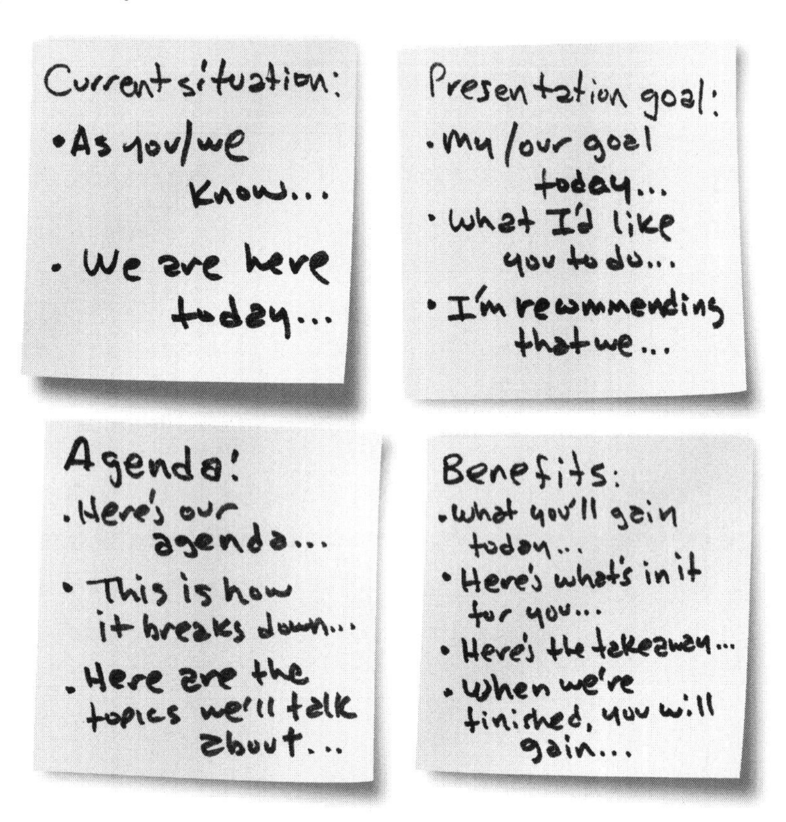

When Terry tried his introduction a second time, it flowed much better. Here's what he said.

State of the IT Unit at BakleTech

Annual Meeting

Terry Kempfert

***As we all know,** we're here for the State of the Unit presentations. I'm here to talk about IT.*

Presentation Goal

- Review current year
- Explain plan for next year

***My goal today** is to review the current year and explain the plan for next year.*

Agenda

This year
- Successes
- Challenges
- Budget to date

Next year
- Goals
- Resources needed
- Proposed budget

***So here are the topics we'll be talking about.** I've divided my agenda into two parts. First, I'll review this year and discuss our successes, challenges, and the budget to date. Second, I'll lay out my goals for next year, the resources needed, and the proposed budget.*

Benefits

- Clear understanding of the plan

***When we're finished, you will gain** a clear understanding of the plan.*

Transitional phrases such as the ones Terry used helped him get to the point quickly and stay focused.

Name the Benefits Up Front: Michael. Michael likes to play with imagery, so after he put his ideas together, he went in search of some graphics.

His reaction to the exercise was interesting. He said that as a sales guy, he is very comfortable with articulating the benefits of his products, but he had never considered talking about them in the introduction. He said he wanted to lead with a benefit. Here's how it went. His stickies looked like this.

Benefits
Successful holiday season

Current Situation
Holidays are coming up, Healthy Summer was a hit.

Presentation Goal
Build on previous success and grow incremental sales with Healthy Holiday promotion

Agenda
1. Promotion overview
2. Coupons + displays
3. Schedule

Michael's first pass at delivering his introduction went like this.

Hey Colleen, let's talk about making the upcoming holidays really successful for you.

As you know, they're coming right up, and Healthy Summer was a huge hit.

So my goal today is to build on that success and grow your incremental sales with our new Healthy Holiday promotion.

We'll talk about three things:

1. *The promotion overview*
2. *The coupons and displays*
3. *The schedule*

By starting with the benefit—holiday success—Michael made his presentation more persuasive.

Naming a Negative Current Situation: Sophia and Elaine. Sophia and Elaine will both face difficult groups, one an internal group of reluctant trainees and the other, a group of skeptical community members. In both cases, the best tactic is dealing with the negativity head-on.

Sophia has two people in her audience who don't like Member Service 2.0 and don't want to attend the training on it. Sophia wants to prevent them from spreading their negativity to the rest of the group. She struggled with the idea of having to acknowledge their attitude at all.

She also struggled to craft the training goal and benefits in a way that would earn her listeners' buy-in. Eventually, she figured it out. Here's what she ended up with.

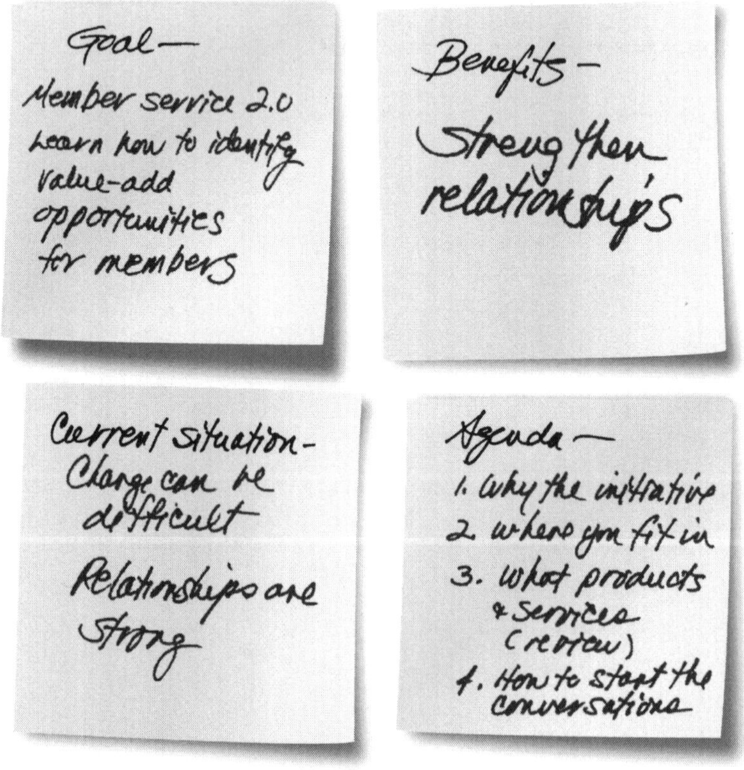

Goal—
Member service 2.0
Learn how to identify value-add opportunities for members

Benefits -
Strengthen relationships

Current situation-
Change can be difficult

Relationships are strong

Agenda —
1. Why the initiative
2. Where you fit in
3. What products & services (review)
4. How to start the conversations

As we've seen, Sophia likes icebreakers and other techniques to loosen up her learners. While she agreed not to use a joke to start things off, she wouldn't let go of animation in her slides. She liked the idea of using stickies, so she kept them for her framing slides. They arrive with an audible swoop, one at a time.

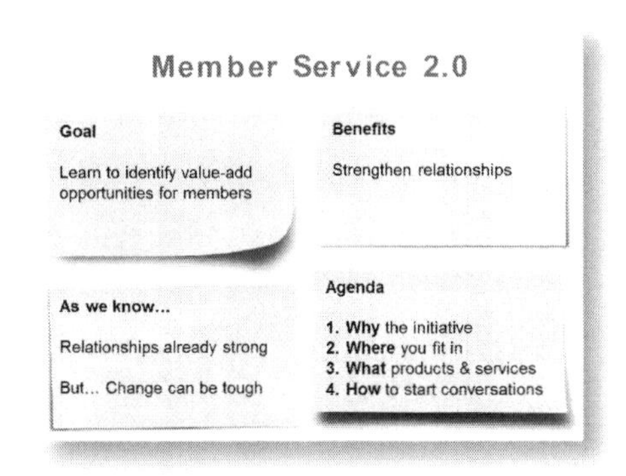

Good morning everyone.

Thanks for joining me for Member Service 2.0.

The goal for today is to learn to identify value-added opportunities for our members.

The benefits for you are strengthened relationships with members.

Now as we all know, your relationships are already strong, and we also know that change can be tough, so that's why we dedicated a day to work through everything.

The agenda looks like this: why the initiative, where you fit in, what products and services we provide (this is just a review, don't worry!). We'll finish the day with some conversation starters.

"With that as your introduction, you don't need an icebreaker," said Jennifer. The group agreed.

While Sophia isn't quite convinced that this introduction will work, she agreed to keep it as is.

Elaine won't know what her situation is until she gets to the site and reads the mood of the group. "However," she said, "if I acknowledge that they love their neighborhood and don't want it to lose its charm, maybe I can diffuse some of the emotion early on." This was a good insight for Elaine. The current situation is often the elephant in the room, the thing no one is brave enough to acknowledge. But if Elaine can start out by recognizing their concern, she is likely to appear empathetic, which will serve her well as she moves through her presentation.

Elaine doesn't normally use slides, because she can never be sure what kind of setup will be available to her. "I think I'll create slides for now but print them out to use as my notes. What I've created here is much better than what I normally have, which is a stack of handwritten note cards. This format helps me be concise and trim the words down to the bare minimum, which is a good thing."

You'll also notice that ultimately, she eliminated the benefits slide because she felt it was redundant and unnecessary given how she had written her goal.

Here's what she said:

Currently

Concerns about neighborhood preservation
&
Questions about rezoning

Hello, everyone. It's wonderful to see so many people here tonight. I know you're probably here for lots of reasons. For one, you might have concerns about the preservation of your historic neighborhood here in Egelton. People always have questions about how zoning works.

Tonight's Goal
Alleviate Your Concerns

Agenda
Jobs & Tax Revenue
Neighborhood Vitality
Virtual Tour
Timeline

I'm here to alleviate your concerns and to convince you that we intend to serve the community well.

I'll do that by showing you the number of jobs we'll create and the resulting tax revenues. We'll take a look at neighborhood vitality, I'll take you on a virtual tour of the plans and show you how we're maintaining the historic look of the neighborhood, and finally I'll roll out a timeline.

We want you to understand that by building new, we can restore the community to its historic past.

"I like this!" said Elaine immediately afterward. Most everyone agreed, except Luis. He brought up a great point about the order of her agenda.

Luis said that if he were in the audience, he'd be skeptical. "If I were a frustrated community member, I wouldn't feel as if you're addressing my needs. I don't think you should lead with jobs and tax revenue. Those are good things, but they don't address the emotion these people are feeling."

As Dale said earlier, it's often appropriate to order your agenda to reflect your audience's concerns. What are they most interested in or concerned about? Put that information first.

Elaine reconfigured the content and order of her agenda. Now it is much more focused on her audience. Here's how it went the second time through.

Currently

Concerns about neighborhood preservation
&
Questions about rezoning

Good evening, everyone. As we know, Egelton is a historic gem. You wouldn't be here tonight if you didn't love the community. I know that you probably have some concerns about preserving it as we make plans to build a mixed-use space across from the library. You may also have questions about rezoning.

Tonight's Goal
Alleviate Your Concerns

Agenda
Virtual Tour
Community Benefits
Economic Impact
Timeline

My goal for tonight is to address your concerns and show you the plans that have been approved by city council.

I'll start by taking you on a virtual tour, I'll lay out some benefits to the community, and time permitting, I'll lay out the economic impact to the community and show you the timeline.

It's my hope that you'll see the benefits, and I'll alleviate your concerns.

"Much better," said Luis. The group agreed.

Using a One-Slide Introduction: Dorothy. Dorothy needed her visuals to serve as projected slides and as a handout for both her live and virtual audiences. To be ecofriendly, she wanted to trim her deck down to the bare minimum. Her solution for the introduction was to put everything on one slide.

Here are Dorothy's stickies:

AGENDA —
1. MOST RECENT DATA
2. SALES PROMOTIONS + RESULTS
3. COMPETITOR ANALYSIS
4. TRENDS
5. FIRE

Benefits—
BETTER
EQUIPPED FOR
SALES
CALLS

Here's how Dorothy's stickies translate to a one-slide introduction. She did a nice job, and if she delivers this slide well to her sales teams, they will be more likely to follow along.

Market Research: October

Goal:
Provide newest data

Agenda:
1. Most recent data
2. Sales promotions & results
3. Competitor analysis
4. Trends
5. Sedgwick fire talking points

Why:
So you are better equipped for your sales calls

Hello, everyone. Thanks for joining me today for our market research meeting.

The goal, as always, is to provide you with the newest market data.

We'll cover five items today. First, the most recent data; second, sales promotions and results; third, the competitor analysis; and fourth, the trends I'm seeing. Finally, we'll work through some talking points for dealing with questions about the Sedgwick fire. When we're done, you'll be better equipped for your sales calls.

"I like the way you numbered your agenda, and then said each number. It helped me follow along," said Terry.

Making Internal Transitions: James. James's case is different from the rest. He's being asked to participate in someone else's presentation, and he didn't like this exercise very much. He said it felt forced and as if he were just checking off things on a list.

It's interesting that James would feel like this. In a way, that's what an introduction should be—a list of things to talk about and a reason for doing it today. But since his introduction is a transition from the previous speaker, we needed to modify it a bit. Here's what James came up with, and eventually he agreed that it was a good way to pick up from the previous presenter.

> "Kim just talked about the features and benefits of adopting our system (current situation). Sometimes people find it helpful to understand the evolution of our method (goal), so I'll give a little history of our successes with other customers and what's led us here today (agenda)."

How Long Should the Introduction Be?

There are, of course, no rules about how long your introduction should be. It simply needs to be long enough for you to provide a sense of direction and purpose and a reason to participate, which in most cases, can be accomplished in under 60 seconds. If you find yourself exceeding two minutes, you may need to rethink how much detail you're going into.

Expanding on the Current Situation: Michael. If your audience's current situation is complex and requires a lot of explaining, consider making it your first agenda point. In Michael's case, his current situation is that the summer promotion was a huge hit. If he and Colleen hadn't previously talked through those details, he should add an agenda point first thing to address them in detail.

Internal Agendas Are Framing Slides: Sophia. The frame doesn't stop with the introduction. The structure that you set up at the beginning should be reinforced throughout the presentation. One way to do this is to use your agenda slide throughout.

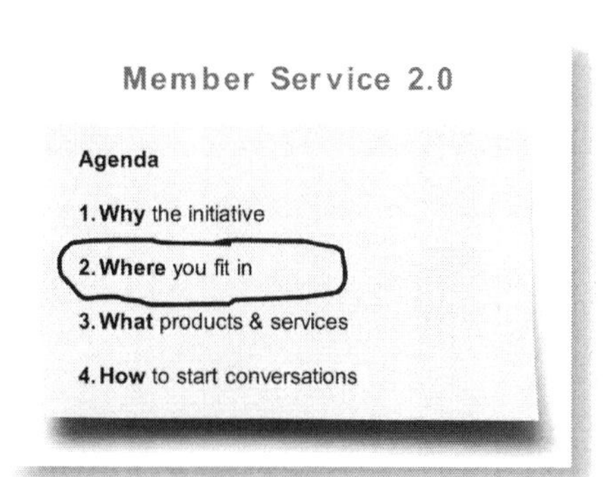

Internal agendas are a great way to keep the conversation on track. Sophia liked the structure they brought to the process and used them in her presentation.

As you can see, the circles simply move down the list as she moves through her presentation.

Create a Framing Slide for the Conclusion

As we mentioned earlier, it's important to create a strong, decisive conclusion. Besides stating clearly that things are just about done, it should also turn over ownership of the information to your listeners.

The slide you use to do this is also considered a framing slide, and should contain a clear, concise summary and at least one action step. Also, the conclusion should contain no new information.

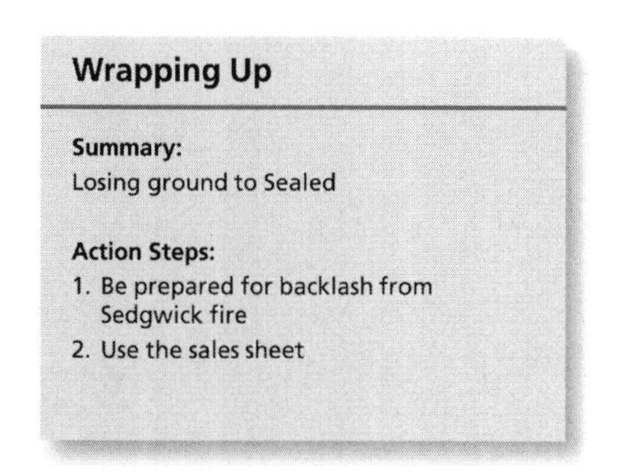

This is Dorothy's conclusion slide. It does a nice job of summarizing the conversation, and her action steps are clear.

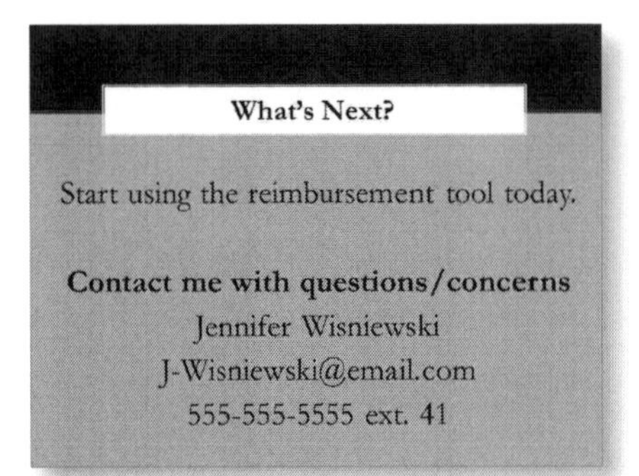

Here's Jennifer's conclusion. It sets a clear action step.

In both cases, the presenters are turning ownership over to their audience members.

So What Does This Mean for You?

If you are like most presenters, creating the frame is far more difficult to get right than any other part of the presentation. It involves these challenges:

1. **You need to look at information you're familiar with from another's perspective.** To succeed, you must focus on what's important to your audience, accept their level of understanding, and do your best to understand attitudes that aren't your own.
2. **Stating your recommendation or goal up front (a deductive approach) may feel counterintuitive.** It's important to frame the presentation so that it's clear from the very beginning where the conversation is going and what you want your audience to do with the information.
3. **Acknowledging negative attitudes and problems can be uncomfortable.** By talking through the current situation, you're creating common ground. You know there's a problem, and by stating it you're saying, "We're in this together. Let's fix it."
4. **A good introduction requires saying things that seem obvious to you.** The temptation to ignore or shortchange them is huge. Don't. Your audience is probably going to be distracted; don't make it worse by asking them to guess what your point is.

5. **You may need to make adjustments at the last minute.** As you know, it's impossible to anticipate every change that could possibly take place between preparation and delivery. These changes can be anything from a minor tweak to a major adjustment. When this happens, let people know right up front that you'll be making changes on the fly based on the new situation.
6. **Using internal agendas may seem unnecessary.** But for long, complex presentations, they provide structure. What you're saying is "here's where we've been, and here's where we still have to go."
7. **Stating the action step in the conclusion may feel as if you're being too bossy or forward.** Audiences appreciate knowing what you want from them. If you're feeling too bossy, soften the words you use.

Although the frame often takes more time to prepare than you think it should, it's worth it. Once it is completed, the body of the presentation falls easily into place. The process involves organizing information so that it follows your agenda, elaborating on the current situation if necessary, and making sure that the connection between what you're presenting and what the audience will gain from it is clear.

Now, we'll look at the visuals you use in the body of your presentations.

Contents

Chapter 10
Create Content Slides

In this chapter . . .

- **Content Slides Are the Subject of the Conversation**
- **Adapting to Your Default Approach**
- **Slides Should Make Your Job Easier**
- **So What Does This Mean for You?**

Dale:

In the afternoon of the first day of our workshops, we sit down and talk about the slides the presenters have prepared. At the beginning of these conversations, we hear a lot of apologies. "Sorry, I know this is a complicated slide, but I included it because..." Or maybe, "Now I know you're not going to like this, but this spreadsheet is important because..."

They don't need to worry. We aren't the PowerPoint police, and we won't be confiscating anyone's slides. Experience has taught us that sometimes presenters have to use slides that are, by any design standard, really lousy. When we see this type of slide, our job is to figure out the best way to communicate what needs to be communicated. Often that has to do with simplifying or altering the slide, but sometimes it has to do with leaving the slide as it is and focusing on how it will be explained during delivery.

Content Slides Are the Subject of the Conversation

The visuals in the body of your presentation are content slides. They deliver the information and ideas that are the subject of the conversation. As we've discussed, these visuals are not limited to PowerPoint. They might be demos, charts, posters, samples, drawings, spreadsheets, and so on. Presenters make choices about what visuals to use based on what the audience needs or wants to see and how much time the presenter has to prepare.

Sometimes this process leads to using visuals pulled from other sources. You may not, for example, have time to turn reports or spreadsheets into simple, streamlined slides, even if you wanted to. Or, you may not have control over the type of slides or level of detail your audience wants to see. We once helped a group of presenters deliver PowerPoint slides divided into four quadrants, each quadrant a separate PowerPoint slide, full of data. They had no choice in the matter. It's what leadership wanted.

In these situations, the question presenters need to ask is not "What's the best way to communicate an idea visually?" but rather, "How can I use this particular visual to make my point?"

While it's easy to say the best slides are the simplest—and we do work with presenters to simplify their slides as much as possible—simplicity is not the goal, understanding is. Sometimes a complex idea can best be explained through the use of a complex image.

We know this goes against most slide design recommendations. I'm sure you've heard there's a "right" number of bullet points to have on a slide and a "right" number of words per bullet. For many presenters, these recommendations are distracting and not very helpful. Decisions about visuals have to be made in the context of each presentation, each audience, and the work to be accomplished.

Just as you can't rehearse your way to success, you can't design your way there either.

This is another way that presenters need to avoid thinking about the process like speechmakers do. The slides you use are not part of a finely honed performance, they are part of a conversation. If the slide on the screen isn't useful to you or the audience in that moment, it's not an effective visual, no matter how well it's designed.

So, just as you can't rehearse your way to success, you can't design your way there either.

Adapting to Your Default Approach

As you develop the content slides for the body of your presentation, it is important to keep your Default in mind. Many of your natural responses and habits need to be kept in check. For example, if you're a Writer, your challenge is to let go of some of the control you want to exert, which means creating visuals that will help you be more flexible and spontaneous during delivery. Improvisers need to create slides that will help them stay focused. Their slides should make it easy for them to communicate the structure listeners need. As you probably expect, initially these adjustments feel uncomfortable. But they lead to positive results.

On the following pages are some graphics illustrating the path to improvement for Writers and Improvisers during preparation.

WRITERS

- "I like to be thorough and accurate."
- "I can always use more preparation time."
- "I want my slides to be perfect."

Which leads to:

Too much faith in preparation

Too much desire for complete control

Analysis paralysis

The desire to include everything you know about your topic

Overuse of slide transitions and animation

Scripting (memorization, desire for notes)

Adjustments:

Include less information on your introductory slides than you'd like

Use your preparation time to simplify, not complicate your slides

Edit bullet points until you think they're too short

Think about concise explanations

Think about alternative ways to explain ideas

Which may feel as if:

- "I am not being accurate."
- "These slides don't have enough detail on them."
- "I have to have notes."

But will lead to:

Clear, easy-to-follow structure

Appropriate level of detail

IMPROVISERS

- "I'm naturally comfortable with my audience."
- "I'm flexible and like a loose organizational structure."
- "I trust myself to be engaging."

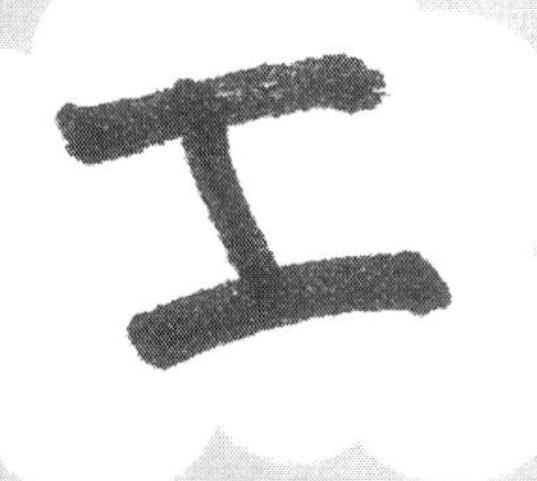

Which leads to:

Delayed preparation
OR
Trouble settling on a single organizational approach, constantly trying out new ways to present information

Slides that are inadequately prepared or inappropriate for this presentation

Adjustments:

Remember that the primary purpose of your slides is to keep you on track

Include more introductory slides than you think you need

Make sure your slides are specific and accurate

Create short, meaningful slide titles

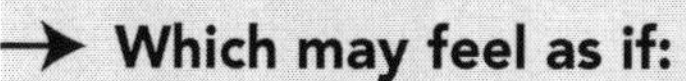

- "I'm committing to slides that may not work."
- "My slides are going to get in my way."

But will lead to:

Clear, easy-to-follow structure

Appropriate level of detail

These pathways always get people talking, because they recognize themselves and the challenges they've faced. It's important to remember that everyone's path to improvement will be different, and it won't always be comfortable, but understanding your Default is an important step along the way.

Here's what our workshop participants said.

The Writers

Sophia

I've always assumed that if I'm prepared and the training content is memorized, I'll succeed. This exercise is showing me that's not necessarily the case. I think I can see the benefit of thinking of "alternative ways to explain ideas." But wouldn't that just mean that I would have several scripts in my head, and I'd have to figure out which one to use? I think that would complicate things too much.

Jennifer

I'm a perfectionist. Like Sophia, I like the idea of thinking of alternate ways to explain the ideas. But I don't think that means I'd have more scripts running through my head. I think alternate explanations would give me more flexibility. Which might help me manage questions?

Terry

Whoa. "The desire to include everything you know about your topic..." That's certainly me, telling the executives how to build the clock. And, as the graphic says, including less would feel less accurate. But then, later it says it will lead to an "appropriate level of detail." At a certain level all of this makes sense, but it's not going to be easy. My introduction earlier was concise, so maybe I can learn from that.

Elaine

I don't think of myself as a control freak, but "Too much desire for complete control" does fit me, at least as far as these town halls go. I've always assumed that I should go in with a controlled message, and they should sit there listening until I'm done, which, of course, doesn't happen.

Sophia and Jennifer both brought up thinking about alternate ways to explain ideas. For Sophia, it seemed as if she'd have to manage more scripts. That is, of course, not the idea we're going after. Instead, we mean that rather than working on finding the one perfect explanation (which of course doesn't exist), it's better to think of different approaches for explaining each concept. Examples include imagining the audience knows a lot about your topic, imagining they know nothing, or imagining they hold incorrect assumptions. Maybe you have only 30 seconds instead of 3 minutes. Thinking this way will help you be more flexible and spontaneous once the conversation is taking place.

Jennifer is correct in thinking that having alternate ways to explain concepts will allow her to be more spontaneous and manage interruptions. Those were things she struggled with because they pulled her out of her script. This realization was a big deal for Jennifer and will help Terry too. It will also help you, especially if you struggle with information overload or the desire to be perfect.

Back to Terry and his comment about his desire to include everything he knows. He's right. Paring down information to be more clear and concise is difficult, but to succeed in his position, he'll need to master it.

The Improvisers

"I trust myself to be engaging." I do. That probably sounds sort of arrogant, but it does come naturally to me. I like it when people ask questions, and as the assessment says, "If I could make them that way, my presentations would be nothing but a series of questions and answers." That would be an ideal situation for me, but I can see how that could be confusing to some people who need more structure. I can also see how it has led to my not having time to close the sale.

"I'm committing to slides that may not work." That's for sure. One of the things that Kim keeps telling me is that I talk about things that aren't relevant to where we are in the sales cycle. She refuses to put in a slide about our history. But I think the company history is important. I feel a strong need to talk about it somewhere, so I do. I just don't have a slide for it.

It also says, "Remember that the primary purpose of your slides is to keep you on track." Does that mean that it's okay to improvise, as long as you keep it about what's on the slide? So that means I should create a slide for our history?

I never thought of it this way, but I have trouble settling on a single way to explain something. Thinking about my decks, I have multiple slides saying the same thing, just from different angles. When it comes to market research, you can slice and dice the data in a lot of different ways. And I do, for goodness sake! This is probably one of the things the salespeople find confusing. In my desire to tell them everything, they're hearing nothing.

LUIS

I'm not a procrastinator, but I did wait until the very last moment on my last presentation. The thing is, school came easy to me. I always assume that business should too. But it doesn't. So because I didn't put enough thought into that presentation, I didn't know what I wanted to say, and it showed. This slide title thing might help. I should craft carefully worded slide titles, then use them to keep me on track without moving into other topics and looping around as I tend to do.

Michael was on to something when he said he'd like to turn his presentations into a series of questions and answers. His ability to engage his buyer in the conversation is a strength, but it can also lead to time management problems. Closing the sale in the allotted time is not about stifling the conversation; it's about managing it better.

James is on to something, too. He'd been fighting his slides, creating a disconnect between what he was saying (the company history) and what was on the screen (one of Kim's slides). There are really two issues here. First, there's the question of whether the company's history should be included in the presentation at all. That is something he and Kim will have to work out. Second, there's his question about whether it's okay to improvise within the confines of the slide. The answer to that question is yes.

Luis is right about slide titles. Figuring out what he wants to say and then creating slides and well-crafted titles is crucial for him. It's very telling that he said school came easy to him, but business does not. I hope the work we did in class will benefit him in this new business environment.

As the pathway graphics show, and as some of the class participants mentioned, adapting to your Default will not be easy, because its influence is strong. We'll see how everyone manages that process in the next chapter when we focus on delivering slides during the presentation, but first we need to talk about creating the slides themselves.

Slides Should Make Your Job Easier

When creating your content slides, keep your needs and your audience's needs in mind. For your audience, information should be as easily understood as possible. For you, the slides you create should be easy to deliver. They should keep you focused and spark the right thoughts when they come up on the screen. That requires anticipating the moment of delivery during preparation. We have several ideas to help you do that.

Crafting Useful Slide Titles: Luis

Effective slide titles are a framing technique, but rather than framing the entire conversation (as the introduction does), they frame the content of individual slides.

While delivering your slides, you should be able to glance at each title and be reminded of what you want to talk about on that particular slide. That means you need to create your titles with an eye on delivery.

As you can see in the following examples, taking extra care with slide titles makes a big difference.

Generic versus Specific. Luis said during the Default discussion that slide titles might help him. He's right, but it took a few tries to get him there. When I sat down with him, he showed me this slide, which was titled "Gross Sales."

While Gross Sales does a fine job of explaining what the graph shows, it doesn't do much else to tee up a story *about* the gross sales. Once the conversation starts, especially if he's disengaged or nervous, he might have a hard time saying much more about this slide.

I asked Luis, "So what? Why should the VC care about your gross sales?"

He answered, "Because we're showing month-over-month growth."

"So maybe that should be your slide title."

He agreed. The second slide is what he came up with. It's much more specific and useful to him, because it frames the conversation well. It says: "We're going to talk about month-over-month sales growth."

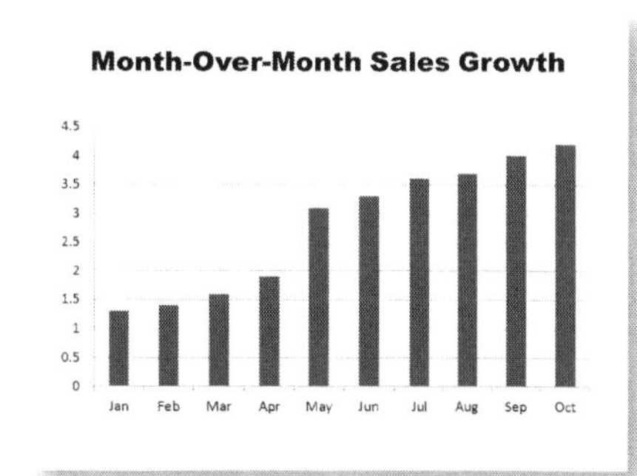

"That's a very different conversation, and one your VC's will be more interested in," I told him.

"That's true," he said, "But this chart also shows a sales bump in May that is pretty impressive, and I could talk about that. I could also talk about the trending assumptions going into next year."

Trigger the Right Thoughts. Luis played around trying to figure out how he wanted the conversation to go. This slide helps him talk about the marketing that took place in the spring and what they're doing to replicate its success.

The oval on the revised slide is a thought trigger. When Luis delivers this slide, the oval will draw his attention to the jump between April and May and remind him to explain it. Thought triggers are an example of making it easy for yourself once the conversation begins.

When Luis talked this slide through, he said something like, "This slide is showing that we've experienced month-over-month sales growth (slide title) since January of this year. As you can see, our growth May over April (thought trigger) was the most dramatic bump so far. It was due to a marketing campaign we put in place in April. We launched a similar campaign this month to see if we can repeat it. The preliminary numbers look promising so far."

"That worked well, I think," I said.

He nodded, then said, "Question for you: would this be a logical time to bring the CMO into the conversation? I could have him talk about the campaign he launched."

I was glad Luis was thinking about his co-presenters. "That's a great idea. Just make sure you prep him in advance. It will be a great way to demonstrate teamwork and to build his credibility when he's answering marketing questions. You should think about bringing the CTO into the conversation as well."

Use a "So What" Text Box. Luis continued tinkering with this slide. This time he wanted to take the conversation in a new direction, talking about what the future holds.

Since his existing chart didn't allow him to look too far forward, I recommended that he add a "so what" text box.

As you can see, this version of the slide prompts an entirely different conversation. I asked Luis to talk it through; here's what he said: "Here you can see we've had consistent month-over-month sales growth (slide title) all year. As the bottom of the slide says, (so-what text box) this positive trending leads our analysts to believe that it will continue next year."

Again, this is a very different conversation.

Luis needs to figure out which story (or stories) is more likely to get a positive response from the VC and continue honing his slides to support his decision.

The really good thing for Luis, one of our Improvisers, is that he now understands how to craft a slide to support the conversation he wants to have. I'm hoping that this will make things easier for him in the future.

Simplify Text: Jennifer

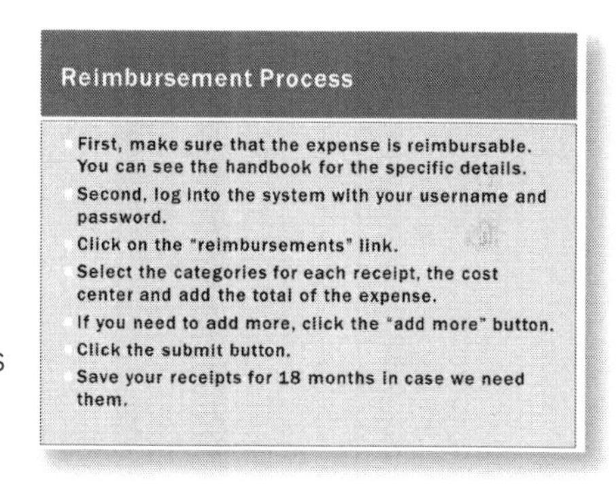

Here are some other ideas to help you create visuals that will make understanding easy for your audience and delivery easy for you.

Let's take a look at one of Jennifer's original slides. As you can see, it's very wordy and would be challenging for anyone to deliver well. It has 81 words, 7 bullets, all full sentences.

Jennifer is a Writer, so it's not surprising that she's created this slide. If you're a Writer, you may have created something similar.

In class, we worked with Jennifer to make her slides easier to use once the conversation begins.

Here's how this slide evolved.

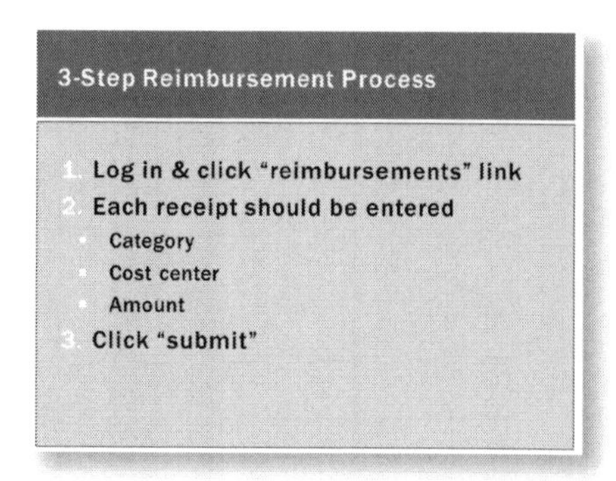

First Edit: Fewer Words. Jennifer did a good job of trimming this slide down to the bare minimum. The process was difficult for her, but she finally made peace with it.

She also improved the slide title.

And the overall effect? The information on the slide was easier for her to deliver and less overwhelming for her listeners. However, when I asked her to talk it through, she stumbled on the second bullet. Because the bullets don't start with the same part of speech, they don't flow well when delivered.

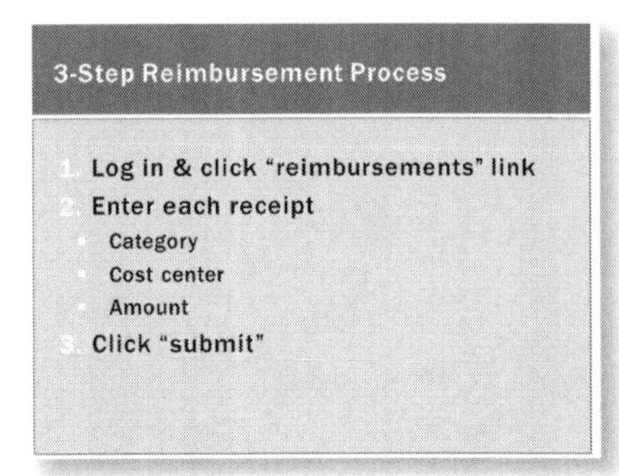

Second Edit: Parallel Bullets. The next task, then, was to make the wording of her bullets parallel. Jennifer decided to begin each step with a verb.

Here's how she delivered this slide. "The reimbursement process is really quite simple. Just three easy steps. First, you log in and click the 'reimbursements' link. Second, you enter each receipt, making sure to include the category, cost center, and the amount. Third, click 'submit.' See? Easy."

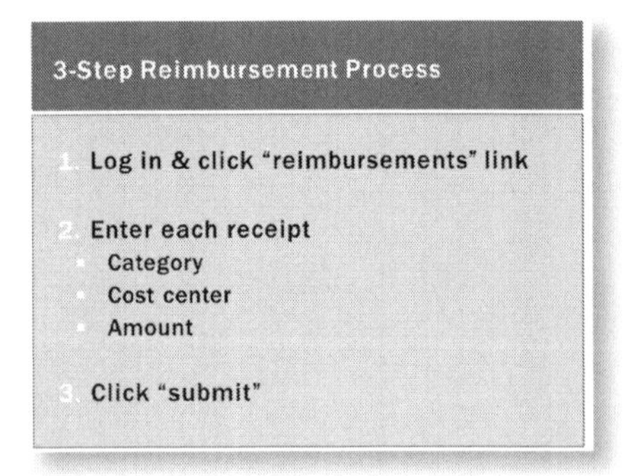

Third Edit: White Space. Jennifer took one more bit of advice. We cleaned it up by adding white space between the top-level bullets. It's a subtle improvement that emphasizes each of the three steps.

Paint a Picture: Elaine

Elaine talked a lot about how important it is to get her listeners to visualize what the future might look like. To help them do that, she has posters that she'll put up around the room.

This poster does a nice job of showing what the neighborhood's future might look like. But it also has to help Elaine manage the conversation. Elaine is a Writer, and if she's like most, she needs a little more than an image to trigger her thoughts.

I recommended that she find at least one word to add to the image. She resisted, saying that she didn't want to lessen the impact of the image.

"Okay, then let's approach it from another angle. You said yesterday that your brain shuts down when things get heated. If that were to happen when you start talking about this image, would you be able to remember what you want to say?"

"Maybe, maybe not," she said.

> **A Word about Licensing Images**
>
> **Be sure that you understand your responsibility for licensing images from online image banks or image searches.**

"Try starting with a statement that simply explains what the image is. Say, 'What we're looking at is . . .' and then finish the sentence."

She tried that and liked it. "I don't want to get a script rolling through your head, but a good transition statement like that can pull you back if your brain shuts down," I said.

Clarify Graphics: Terry

When Terry initially showed me this slide, I had a hard time figuring out what it was, so I asked him.

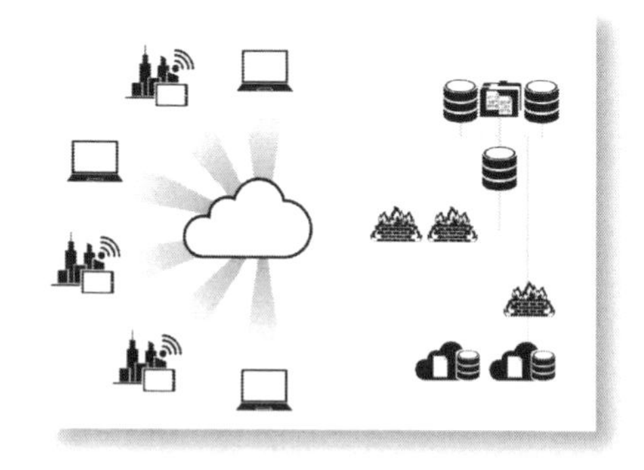

"It's a process map showing how data is stored in the primary data center and is backed up in the secondary data center. It also shows how data moves securely through firewalls, up to the cloud, and back down to our locations worldwide.

"That's a lot of information. Answer this question as concisely as you can: 'For this specific audience, at this point in time, what's the takeaway?'"

Terry thought about it and finally said, "We have a global process in place that keeps our information confidential, and it's backed up in case of disaster."

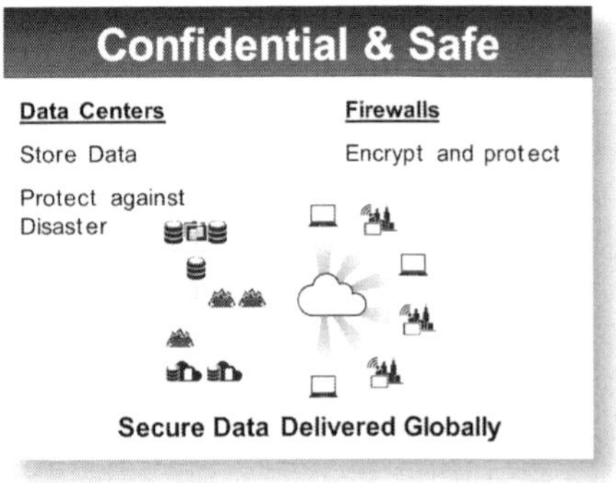

"Great, let's make this slide support that takeaway."

The first thing we did was flip the image so that the process moves from left to right. This makes it easier to grasp, since we read left to right. Then we labeled the map to emphasize the benefits.

The slide isn't going to win any design awards, but it does a better job supporting Terry's conversation. As Dale said, if a well-designed visual doesn't support the conversation, it's not doing its job.

If a well-designed visual doesn't support the conversation, it's not doing its job.

Simplify Spreadsheets

There's no getting around it. Sometimes, you have to use spreadsheets in your presentation. They are a necessary part of getting business done, so don't shun them. However, they do need special attention if they're going to be delivered well. Here are some ideas to consider.

- If you can, trim back information not critical to your message.
- Identify a single story you want the spreadsheet to support. If there are multiple stories, much like Luis's bar graph, create a separate slide for each story.

- Bring focus to the story by adding a thought trigger. Highlighting a row or making the numbers in particular cells bold are two good ways to do that.

When Slides are also Documents

Michael and Dorothy both asked what to do when your slide deck also serves as a leave-behind document. This is a challenge. On one hand, your slides need to support the conversation; on the other hand, the hard copy needs to include enough context to make sense later or to inform someone who wasn't able to attend the presentation. Here are a few ideas to consider.

1. Create your slides to support the conversation. In other words, take the less-is-more approach. Later, add context and details in the speaker notes. When you print the handout, print it with the slide at the top of the page, with the notes down below.

2. Add a so-what text box to each slide, as Luis did. Make sure that it's crystal clear and cannot be misunderstood later. Using this method will build in a safety net for your conversation. Forget your point? Look to the so-what box.
3. Create a second version of the deck that includes context and detail. Use your slide deck to support the conversation while giving your listeners the more detailed paper version.

4. Create the slide as if it were a stand-alone document; add thought triggers to focus everyone's attention.

Adapting Slides You Didn't Create

Delivering visuals created by others can be difficult. First, the act of organizing your own content helps you get the information set in your mind. When you don't create your own content, information does not take root as quickly or strongly. Second, if we agree that visuals spark your thoughts, delivering someone else's slides may not spark the right thoughts for you. When you're delivering someone else's slides, do what you can to make them your own. If nothing else, work with the slide titles and add thought triggers to pull your attention to the right spot.

Avoiding Distractions

Be careful of getting too fancy. When PowerPoint first came out, it was a lot of fun to add builds and animations. Remember the "whooshing" sound from Sophia's introduction? Avoid anything that calls too much attention to itself. If your listeners are distracted by an animation or how clever your slides are, they're focused on the wrong things, and you've failed to make understanding easy.

So What Does This Mean for You?

Well-designed visuals do more than provide information; they bring order to the conversation. As you put together the body of your presentation, remember that while design is important, your slides have two main purposes: to make it easy for you to deliver the message as well as help your audience to grasp the content. That requires keeping your Default in mind and anticipating the moment of delivery.

Well-designed visuals do more than provide information; they bring order to the conversation.

In the next chapter, we'll look at ways to use the visuals you've created once the conversation starts.

Contents

Chapter 11
Manage the Conversation

In this chapter . . .

- **Show the Audience Where to Look**
- **Talk about What They're Seeing**
- **Provide Context**
- **Defaults during Delivery**
- **Here's What Presenters Learned from Their Videos**
- **So What Does This Mean for You?**

When you deliver your presentations, your attention will—and should—be pulled in two directions: toward the plan you created in advance and toward the conversation taking place at the moment. The tension between the two plays out differently for everyone.

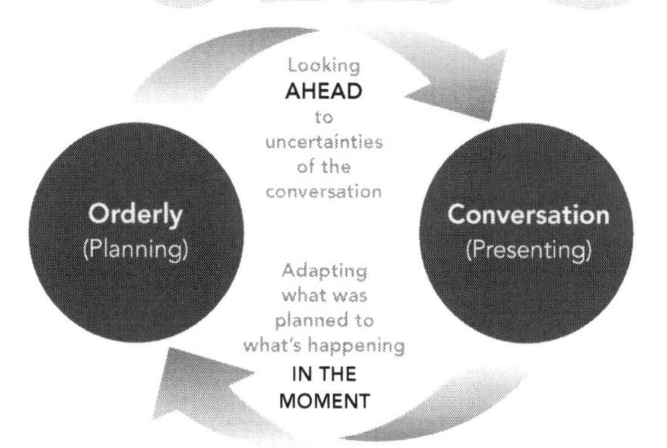

To illustrate this idea, let's take a look at what happened to one of our presenters. Dorothy was delivering her presentation in front of the class. Things were rolling along just fine when she brought up the next slide in her deck, looked at it, and froze. For some people, this sort of freeze lasts for just a second or two. For Dorothy it was longer. Finally, she turned from the slide to me and said, "I'm sorry. I just lost it. I don't know what to say about this slide."

When this happens, it's not because the presenter doesn't understand what the slide is or what it is meant to communicate. Dorothy knew exactly what she needed to say. Her struggle was in finding the best way to fit the slide into the conversation that was taking place before the slide hit the screen. In her case, the slide was a new topic, one that required a big shift in the flow of the conversation.

Presenters usually feel bad when this happens, sometimes even a little foolish. I tell them, though, that it's perfectly natural. After all, when you are engaged in a conversation with your audience and things are humming along the way you want them to, the next slide in your deck may not fit effortlessly into the conversation. Sometimes a slide will arrive on the screen like an uninvited guest, demanding your attention. When it does, it simply means that the tension between order and conversation is playing out.

Besides, if this *never* happens to you, you might be suffering from a much larger problem. Here are two examples of what I mean. I'm sure you've seen presenters speak while slides languish on the screen. They may be talking about the content of the slide, but they're ignoring the slide itself. On the other hand, some presenters do nothing but focus on the slides. While what they say may be accurate, they're not engaging their listeners in a conversation.

These approaches are two sides of the same coin. They both assume that slides are capable of doing their work by themselves. One treats the slide as a *parallel* channel of communication, running alongside what's being said without any connection to it. The other treats the slide as the *sole* channel of communication. In neither situation is the slide *part of* the conversation.

Here's the question we'll answer in this chapter: how do presenters stay engaged in the conversation—which requires speaking spontaneously in the moment—while delivering information and visuals they've thought about and created in advance?

The answer is to call attention to what's happening in the moment. That requires three things: (1) showing your audience where to look, (2) talking about what they're seeing, and (3) providing context. Let's look at each technique in detail.

Show the Audience Where to Look

Think about the moment you press the button on the remote to advance to the next slide in your presentation. From both your perspective and the audience's, that moment should be a big deal. Not a world-peace-at-last big deal, but important in terms of the conversation you're having. When that new slide appears, you are taking the next step in your plan. By drawing attention to it, you are reinforcing what makes your presentation orderly. Besides, when the new slide appears on the screen, the audience will naturally shift their attention to it, sometimes just a glance, sometimes more. It would be a mistake not to take advantage of that shift in focus, especially if the conversation has wandered off point on the preceding slide.

Unfortunately, this opportunity is often lost because presenters think they shouldn't look at the slide. As a result, they fail to focus the audience's attention appropriately. But when you look at the slide, when you move to it and point things out, the slide becomes something you're *showing* the audience. Rather than being a parallel channel of communication, running its own course, the slide is the subject of the conversation for as long as you want it to be.

Direct Focus Toward and Away from the Slide

Think about watching local news and weather on TV. Two delivery techniques are being used—one by the newscaster, another by the weather person. The newscaster, let's say his name is Adam, is like a speechmaker. Adam is using a prompter, reading the script as it is projected on a piece of glass positioned in front of the camera lens. Because Adam is good at his job, you can't see his eyes moving across the script, and it feels like he's speaking spontaneously straight into the camera. Often, just to the side of his head is an image that's relevant to the story. It might be a picture of the person Adam is talking about. It might be a logo or some other graphic image. Adam doesn't talk about this image. It's used to help viewers know what the story is about and to punctuate the shift to another story.

Now let's talk about the person delivering the weather. The meteorologist—we'll call her Jill—is not scripted. She speaks off the top of her head, standing in front of a green screen where an image is projected for the viewer—the map, the list of temperatures, the forecast, whatever is appropriate for the moment. As Jill speaks, she points to various things on the wall behind her. She indicates the cold fronts, the temperatures, the moving satellite images. As she does this, we follow along, looking where Jill wants us to look. Jill's presence in the shot is not annoying. She might be standing in front of the Gulf of Mexico when she points to something in Texas, but it doesn't matter because we trust Jill to show us where to look. When she's finished with the visual portion of the weather report, Jill moves away from the image to speak to us through the camera. That's when she sums things up, reminds us to take our umbrellas, and turns things back to Adam.

Jill is doing what presenters need to do. Granted, you're not using a green screen, and you're not speaking to a camera, but the technique Jill uses to direct our attention to an image is the same. When you're delivering a slide, it's best to look at it, move to it, and point things out on it. Then, when you're finished showing your audience what they need to see, you move away from the slide. When you do this, you control the audience's focus and take full advantage of the visual component of your presentation.

The amount of time you spend with each slide will vary, of course. When you're delivering a content slide, it's necessary to focus listeners' attention on it for a longer period of time than when you're delivering a framing slide. The thing to remember is that you are in control of how much attention the slide gets, and when. In this way, the slide contributes to and does not distract from the conversation.

Move with Purpose

Directing focus to and from the screen usually meets resistance from our participants. There are two reasons for this. One has to do with performance rules and the other with being stuck in the funhouse.

First, what we're recommending butts up against some stubborn performance assumptions and rules, as summarized in the accompanying box.

The Rules You Can Break

Never Turn Your Back on the Audience

Moving to the screen may mean turning away from the audience. In some rooms, this means you will be turning your back on them for a few seconds. This is not as big a problem as it seems. When you're moving with purpose and fully engaged with your listeners, you will keep everyone in the conversation.

Laser Pointers Help

Some presenters assume that using a laser pointer is the best way to point things out on a slide. But pointers should be used

The Rules You Can Break (continued)

as an absolute last resort. When you have the freedom to move or when you can describe where you want people to look, put the pointer down. It's not helping you, and, trust me on this, it is annoying your audience.

Glance Down at Your Laptop Screen When Referring to Your Slides
Looking down at your laptop means you aren't looking at your listeners. Granted, if you look very briefly at your laptop, the break in eye contact is minimal. But most presenters don't do that. They get sucked into the monitor, and engagement is lost. Besides, the conversation will feel much more natural and spontaneous when you're looking where your audience is looking.

Of course, there are times when the physical movement we're recommending is not possible or effective. The screen might be very high or far away. The audience's sightlines may be a factor. You may, for whatever reasons, be stuck behind a table or a lectern.

Regardless of the physical limitations of the room, your goal when delivering slides is still the same. You need to direct the audience's focus to the slide and bring it back to you in a controlled, purposeful way. When movement is restricted, you will have to do it using directional language. For example:

- "As you can see in the upper left hand corner of this slide..."
- "Let's move on to the final bullet point on this slide. As you can see there,..."

Direct the audience's focus to the slide and bring it back to you in a controlled, purposeful way.

- "This is a photo taken of the last project we completed at 14 Ways. Moving from left to right, we can see that..."

Now let's get back to the second reason presenters resist movement, which we touched on earlier. Some presenters are simply nervous, and walking back to the screen feels very uncomfortable. They're experiencing a common funhouse effect, and it involves a distorted sense of how far they are moving. We call it getting stuck in no-man's-land. The illustration below shows where you'll find no-man's-land: it's point B, the weakest position in the room, halfway between the screen and the audience.

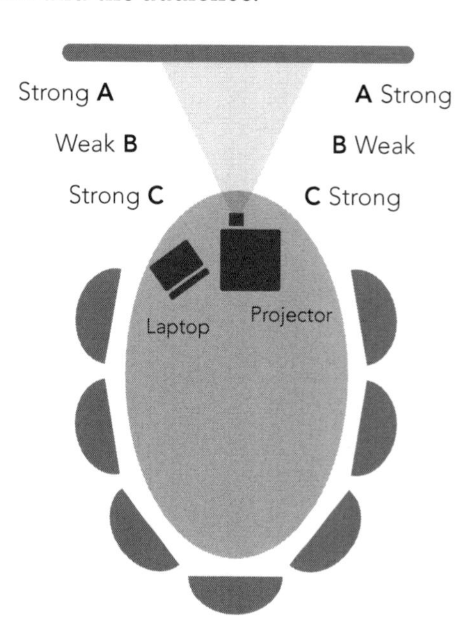

For many presenters, no-man's-land is a comfortable place to be, neither too close to the screen nor too close to the audience. But, if you station yourself there and never move, you'll be forced either to twist around so you can look at the screen or to glance down at your laptop monitor when you need to look at the slide you're projecting. Most people choose to look at the laptop.

The problem with this approach is that you aren't taking advantage of the space you have. When you're at the screen, position A, and pointing things out, listeners know where to look. When you're at C, you strengthen your connection with them, and they will know to focus on you.

Talk about What They're Seeing

As you direct the listeners' focus to the slide, take the time to tell the audience what they're seeing. When a pie chart comes up on the screen, for example, the presenter might be naturally inclined to talk about the point the chart makes, not the fact that the image is a pie chart, that the slices of the pie are different colors, or why a pie chart was chosen to communicate the point in the first place. The presenter assumes that the audience is capable of understanding the slide instantly, and that explaining it is unnecessary. Remember, though, your audience is engaged in a conversation, not simply reading a document. If they were merely reading, they would have all the time they need to understand what the pie chart means. Since they're listening to you, they need guidance.

We encourage presenters to answer the "What is this?" question when a new slide comes up. The easiest way to do that is to refer to the slide title as Luis did with his month-over-month sales growth slide. If you're using product samples, like Michael, it's as easy as saying, "Here are the two new flavors I'd like you to try."

What about Text or Bullet Points?

When it comes to slides that include text or bullet points, many presenters apply what's considered to be the bedrock rule of delivery: *Never read from your slides*. This rule is no doubt the result of too many presenters ignoring their listeners as they drone through unedited bullet points.

Following this rule means that the presenter talks about or summarizes the information in the bullet points without using the same language as the bullets. As he or she does this, the audience reads what's on the screen. As I said earlier, this creates two parallel channels of communication and assumes audience members are capable of listening and reading simultaneously. This doesn't work. But for some reason, we have been told that audiences can pull it off.

Let's look at a non-presentation example. Let's say you're sitting in your office, and a coworker stops by to talk about a report he has just written. He hands you the report and starts talking about it. Let's say the report is really important and you want to understand it. Let's also assume that you want to understand what your coworker is saying about it. In that situation, you would say, "Hold on, let me read this." You would not be able to read carefully and listen well at the same time. It's like texting and driving. We might think we can manage it safely, but we can't.

Successful Bullet Point Delivery Begins during Preparation

As we discussed in a previous chapter with Jennifer's presentation, bullet points have to be easy to read. Here are some recommendations:

- **Shorten them as much as possible, assuming that you will be supplying much of the detail surrounding them during the presentation.**
- **Begin each bullet with the same part of speech.**
- **Read the list aloud as you prepare, just as the way it's written. If the bullets are difficult to read or sound awkward, you'll know they need editing to be more readable.**

I'm not saying reading from the slides—and saying nothing more about them—is a good practice. It's not. But I am saying that presenters need to control when the audience's focus goes to the visual and when it doesn't. Bullet points require reading. This isn't about reading something the audience can read for themselves. It's about focus and the efficient use of the visual. The "never read from your slides" rule often has the opposite effect.

Bullet points require reading. This isn't about reading something the audience can read for themselves. It's about focus and the efficient use of the visual.

Provide Context

Successful delivery means keeping everything in context, and there are two levels of context you need to be aware of. One is about how the presentation fits into the audience's world. As you know, this is communicated during the introduction as you talk about the frame for the presentation. When presenters struggle with delivering the introduction, it's usually because they have forgotten that it's simply about establishing this context. They dive into the details of the presentation prematurely. The transitional phrases we talked about with Terry's introduction are a way to keep this meta-level perspective in mind.

The second type of context is about how the plan is playing out during delivery. Each slide in the body should be placed in the context of the conversation taking place. Sometimes that involves bringing the decisions you made during preparation into the conversation. It might mean, for example, explaining why a slide was included, where it came from, or what's important about it. At other times, it involves connecting dots between the slide on the screen and the interaction you just had with someone about a previous slide. Your slides will not always arrive on the screen at the perfect time. What's important is that you bring the slide into the conversation that's taking place.

The box on this and the following page summarizes some ways our presenters can emphasize context.

Ways to Emphasize Context

What is the "so what" on this slide?

- "The point of this slide is that our promotions have been even more successful than we expected in several key markets."
- "You might be thinking that we shouldn't worry about what the low-end folks are doing. The reality is that it matters because they could, over time, erode the entire category, making low-end roofing the status quo. That would hurt us and our long-term profitability."
- "So as you can see, our growth has been steady and strong."

How does it fit in?

- "We just took a virtual tour of the exterior of the building; now let's look at the interior."
- "Okay, we've talked about the reimbursement process in a general way; now let's get into the details."
- "I touched on the project timeline a couple minutes ago in response to Councilman Rogers's question about not disrupting the annual St. Patrick's Day parade. Here's more about the proposed timeline..."

When was the slide made?

- "When I put this slide together, I didn't have access to all the current data because of the holiday weekend slowing everything down. But, even so, we can clearly see the trend..."
- "This slide is from last quarter. Let's look at it in comparison to where we are today."
- "I pulled this data together this morning. The media are going to have questions for us about the fire-resistant material that failed in last weekend's fire in Sedgwick. It wasn't our roofing, but we do use similar chemicals in our manufacturing process."

Who created the slide?

- "This slide came from our marketing department. It's typically used to compare trends over time with various customers. For our purposes today,..."

Ways to Emphasize Context (continued)

- "I got this slide from our friends in finance. It shows us..."
- "Tyler created this slide, and I borrowed it from him because it does a great job explaining what we've been working on the last two months."

What does the slide mean to various audience members?

- "For those of you in Finance, you can see that my proposed budget for the new IT infrastructure is higher than you probably want. But if we look at it from the Operations and HR point of view, it will save on overhead at each of our global locations."
- "For the Member Service Reps in the room, this means you'll need to listen and ask clarifying questions so that you can identify an opportunity. For the Account Managers, you'll need to jump on these opportunities in a timely manner."
- "Lorelei, I'm glad you're here. As a category manager, you may see some additional opportunities to build awareness for the Healthy Holiday promotion in the checkout lanes."

What does the slide mean to you?

- "From my perspective in marketing, this is a trend that we need to watch because..."
- "When we were planning the new reimbursement process, one of our top priorities was simplicity. I think this slide really shows how we've achieved that goal."
- "When I pulled this data together, I was really proud to see such steady growth."

Let's take a look at how your Default Approach influences slide delivery.

Defaults during Delivery

Just as there's a pathway for adapting to your Default during preparation, there is also one for delivery. In the preparation pathway, we pointed out that many of the recommended adjustments might feel awkward but would lead to effective slides. The same is true here. While the adjustments might not feel good right away, they will lead, as you can see at the bottom of each pathway, to clear, concise explanations and flexible, conversational delivery.

WRITERS

- "I assume that perfect slides ought to lead to perfect delivery."
- "I worry about saying things right."
- "My slides are more important than I am."

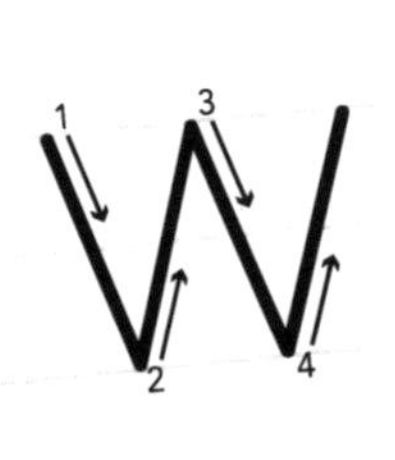

Which leads to:

More attention to slides than listeners

Sense of failure when things don't go according to plan

Adjustments:

Stop trying to say everything perfectly

Use slide titles to pull yourself out of the details

Emphasize big picture ideas from the introduction throughout the presentation

Which may feel as if:

- "I'm not demonstrating my knowledge."
- "I'm not giving enough detail."
- "I'm not being accurate."
- "I'm not doing my job."

But will lead to:

Clear, concise explanations

Flexible, conversational delivery

IMPROVISERS

- "I assume that effective delivery occurs in spite of my slides."
- "I am more interesting and more important than my slides."
- "I hope I can fit in everything I have to say."

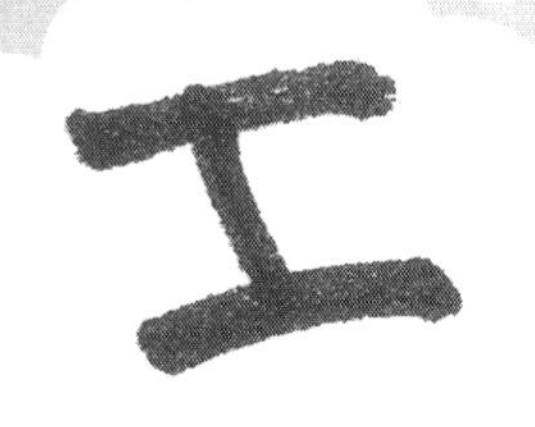

Which leads to:

Long, rambling delivery

Glossing over the logical flow of your presentation

Ignoring slides, getting ahead of what's on the screen

Feeling lost if the audience is not responsive

Adjustments:

Force yourself to pay special attention to the slides in the introduction and conclusion

Feel free to improvise within the limits of the slide you're projecting on the screen

Use the slide titles to keep you on track

Which may feel as if:

- "The slides are getting in my way."
- "This is silly; they can read the slides. I don't need to."

But will lead to:

Clear, concise explanations

Flexible, conversational delivery

After reading through the pathways, here's what the class participants had to say.

The Writers

The adjustment I think I need to work on is "Stop trying to say everything perfectly." That's going to be hard, but you've convinced me that that's what I need to do.

I agree, Sophia—I worry about saying things just right, too. That jumps out at me. And it leads to a "Sense of failure when things don't go according to plan." This is exactly what I described earlier. I stand by what I said; I like the idea of "Thinking of alternative ways to explain ideas," while I prepare. Next, I need to use the slide titles to remind me of what I need to say, then just speak off the cuff. It's such a shift from what I've been doing.

I need predictability, and I think the reason I'm so nervous with the execs is that they aren't predictable at all. Which means I need to get comfortable with the zigging and zagging of the conversation. The thing that jumps out at me is this: if I don't go into a lot of detail, "I'm not demonstrating my knowledge." My job is about the details, or at least it used to be. That said, I think I finally understand what I need to do, and that framing strategy will be key.

I agree with all of you. All of this control I'm trying to exert has led to a "Sense of failure when things don't go according to the plan." Yeah, I need to let that go.

The Improvisers

Michael

This quote jumps out—"I am more interesting and more important than my slides"—resonates with me. I think that statement is absolutely true. I'm the presentation; the slides are just there for backup. Right?

James

Right, speaking comes easily to me too. It always has, so identifying as an Improviser makes sense. And this quote, "My slides are going to get in my way," is exactly how I feel. The other thing that cuts close to the bone is "Long, rambling delivery." I've been accused of that before, and my wife always says "get to the point, you're confusing me." Maybe she's right.

Dorothy

For me, it's all about glossing over the logical flow. I think that's what I've been doing. And this is where those framing slides are going to come in handy. I loved how Sophia used the recurring internal agenda. I'm going to do that too. And with everything else we've talked about, I don't think that "Feeling lost if the audience is not responsive," is going to be a problem anymore.

Luis

I wish I were that confident, Dorothy. "Feeling lost if the audience is not responsive" jumped out at me too, because that's what happened before. The audience sat there stone cold. That's why I was so uncomfortable, and as an Improviser, I just kept going and going and going. I knew I needed to stop talking, but I couldn't. Using the slide titles to focus my message is going to make all the difference, I think. I hope.

The insights everyone had are terrific. By staying focused on these ideas and not slipping back into old habits, each presenter will be more successful.

Here's What Presenters Learned from Their Videos

Following this discussion, the class members delivered their presentations from beginning to end. Afterward, they reviewed their videos with me. Here's a recap of some interesting conversations we had.

Using the Screen: Sophia

Sophia, as you know, holds tight to some performance techniques and rules. During this exercise, she was resistant to turning her back and walking to the screen to point things out. That is, until she saw how ineffective she was when she faced her audience the entire time. She said, "I never realized how much frustration I was causing my learners. On the video, I can see that I completely ignored that decision tree graphic. I don't even think I mentioned what it was. But, when Dale had me deliver it a second time, I walked to the screen and talked them through the details. It made so much more sense."

Sophia's breakthrough on this simple concept is going to significantly improve her training sessions.

Delivering Bullets: Luis

Here's a slide created by Luis. As you can see, he did a nice job making his bullets concise and parallel. Structurally, this is a good slide. It took him awhile to get it to this point, but he sees the benefit in honing his content to the bare minimum.

Outstanding Competitive Advantage

- Technical capabilities are faster
- Sales team is well-connected
- Growth potential is high
- Unique brand and high awareness

There are a few options to consider when it comes to delivering a bullet slide.

Option 1: Read the Entire List. Read through the bullets without comment. After this overview, go back and deliver the details for each point. Here's what Luis said when he followed this recommendation:

> "We have an outstanding competitive advantage. Our technical capabilities are faster, our sales team is well connected, and as we saw earlier, the growth potential is high. Finally, we have a unique brand with high awareness.
>
> Let me talk about each of these in more detail. About the technical capabilities..." He went into more detail with each of the bullets. He said less about the growth potential because he'd already talked about that on an earlier slide.

This option works well when you have a short list and you want to maintain as much flexibility as possible. Using this technique, you could easily decide on the fly to spend more energy on a particular point if you learned someone was particularly interested in it.

Option 2: Go into Detail One at a Time. You could go into the details of each bullet one at a time. Dale asked Luis to give it a try.

> "We have an outstanding competitive advantage. Our technical capabilities are faster than practically anyone else in our industry. For example,..."
>
> "Moving to the next point, the sales team is well connected. John Kyle, as you probably know, came from Sun Star, and he knows just about everybody, which makes him..."
>
> "Our growth potential is high, which is my third point..."

This approach can work well. The risk is that your listeners will read down the list while you're still speaking about the first bullet. As Dale said, no one can read and listen simultaneously, so you may lose focus with this option.

Option 3: Animate the Bullets. To counter the ability of listeners to read ahead, you could bring in the bullets one at a time. This should not be your go-to technique with every list of bullet points, though, because it restricts your flexibility. The bullets appear in the predetermined order and have to be delivered in sequence. Improvisers find this technique especially frustrating because they tend to get ahead of themselves, which is exactly what happened when Luis tried it.

When we reviewed his video, Luis said he liked the first option best. He said reading down the list and going back to fill in the gaps gave him more control. He was also surprised that reading the bullets didn't feel or look odd at all.

Many presenters resist the idea of reading bullet points. James is in this group. However, like Sophia and Luis, he liked what he saw on his video. "There's a connection between what I'm saying and what they're reading. Huh. And it doesn't bother me at all to watch it, even though it felt strange when I did it."

Ordering Bullets: Jennifer

In Jennifer's presentation, the bullets she used were steps in a process. Putting them in the right order, then, was easy. When the order of the bullets is not so obvious, it's often a good idea to explain why the bullets are listed the way they are. Are they organized from most to least important? Chronologically? By region? Providing this information will help your audience know how to think about the content you're delivering.

Trust the Slide: Dorothy

Some presenters struggle with text on slides even when they aren't using bullets. They may try to change it or improve what the slide says as they deliver it. Most of the time this goes back to the maxim of never reading what's on the slide. When presenters do this, though, they confuse themselves and their listeners.

Here's a slide Dorothy struggled to deliver. As you can see, the slide itself is pretty clear. It's a pie chart showing market share with a brief note explaining that AWR, her company, lost two points to its competitor, Sealed. It's a simple slide that should be easy to deliver.

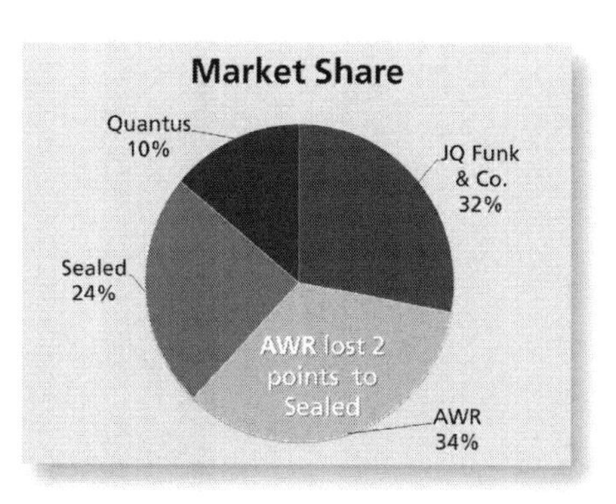

But when the slide came up on the screen, she said, "Let's turn our focus to the uh … the competitive landscape. As you can see, we have 34% share. Sealed took two points from us and uh … sorry, I'm losing it."

If we compare what's on the slide to what Dorothy said, we can see that she changed the language.

- She said "competitive advantage" instead of "market share."
- She also changed the wording when she mentioned Sealed. The slide reads "AWR lost 2 points to Sealed," but what Dorothy said was, "Sealed took two points from us…"

In both instances, she caused confusion for herself and her listeners. Dorothy is an Improviser, so her impulse to invent as she goes along is not surprising. We talked in previous chapters about finding ways to create slides that are easy to deliver. Dorothy's done that with this slide. Her title is solid (although she later decided to make it more specific). The pie chart is labeled. The "so what," which is the white text, is concise and pulls attention to itself. When she delivers the slide, she simply needs to trust it to guide her.

She could have said, "Let's turn our focus to market share. As you can see at the bottom of this pie chart, AWR lost 2 points to Sealed." No confusion there.

When she tried it again, here's how it went.

> "Here we have Market Share." She walked to the screen and pointed to the bottom of the pie chart, "Unfortunately, the news is grim. As you can see, AWR is currently at 34%. While we still enjoy a very healthy slice of the market, we've lost two points to Sealed. She turned to the group and walked toward them through no man's land as she continued talking about how Sealed, the low-end competition, was gaining strength because of an aggressive pricing strategy and its targeted cable television advertising campaign.

Dorothy was much happier with her second attempt. There was a tighter connection between what her audience was seeing and what she was saying. Further, because she directed their focus first to the screen and then back to her, there was no question about where they should look. Her presentation looked and sounded very natural. Her point was clear to the audience: they need to do something about the competition.

We went on to talk about her slide title. I asked her if she could improve it, and she said yes. "It should be something like, 'Troublesome Market Share.'"

Transitions between Slides: Sophia and Luis

Many people worry about delivering smooth transitions. Their thinking goes something like this: "I want my presentation to flow smoothly.

I want my audience to think that I am fully prepared and know exactly how this presentation is going to go. Therefore, I will memorize the order of my slides and the transitions between them."

The problem with this approach is that it goes after the wrong goal. That sort of rehearsed transition may work during a formal speech, but during a getting-business-done presentation, it gets in the way. What you say as you move from slide to slide is an opportunity to remind listeners where the conversation has been, where it's going, and why.

The key to an effective transition is pausing. Pausing between slides gives you time to think, and it gives your audience time to let what you just said sink in. Here are two examples of transitions gone wrong.

The key to an effective transition is pausing. Pausing between slides gives you time to think, and it gives your audience time to let what you just said sink in.

- When Sophia delivered her training to her classmates, she got to the end of one of her slides and then blanked out. She turned to Dale, who was behind the camera, and said, "I can't remember what my next slide is."
- Luis, on the other hand, advanced to his next slide before he finished speaking about the previous one. Here's what happened. He said, "When you look at the strength of our entire enterprise and all of our growth potential, you can see (here's where he advanced his slide) that we will be profitable sooner than originally projected."

Sophia needs to remember that she doesn't always need to know what slide is next. Worrying about that puts too much pressure on presenters and pulls you out of the here and now of the conversation.

Luis made listening difficult. His final words about profitability were very powerful, but when he advanced the slide while saying them, he lessened their impact on the audience.

What could both Sophia and Luis have done differently? Finish their explanation of the slide they were on, advance to the next slide, pause long enough to look to the slide title and gather their thoughts, and then begin speaking.

This technique makes the transition easier for you and strengthens its impact on your audience.

Using a Handout: Michael

Michael will deliver his presentation to Colleen, who will be seated across the desk from him. He'll use a hard copy of his slide deck. Many people assume that this is an easier way to present because it feels less formal. However, once the conversation starts and the handout is in your listeners' hands, you lose a lot of control. Your listeners can (and do) page through the handout any way they want. Use these techniques to keep them focused.

- Tell them what the document is and how you'd like to use it. Will you go through it page by page? Is it primarily a reference for them to use later?
- Give them time to look at the document when you first give it to them. Then redirect their attention to the page you want to focus on.
- Use directional language such as, "in the upper right corner," or "moving on to page 13." This is the verbal equivalent of the weather person showing you the storm pattern over the Gulf of Mexico.

Using Product Samples: Michael and James

Michael and James asked about using product samples. Michael said it's not uncommon for him to take in samples of a new energy bar to let his buyers taste them. James said they sometimes have packaging samples on hand to show potential customers. Using samples is a wonderful way to add value to your presentation. Samples should be treated like handouts. Give people time to look, touch, listen, or taste before you move on in your presentation.

So What Does This Mean for You?

Successful presenters manage the tensions inherent to the Orderly Conversation—the tension between reading and listening and the tension between preparation (then) and delivery (now). They do this by controlling the audience's focus, talking about what the audience is seeing as well as about what it means, and providing the proper amount of context throughout. If you do this, you will successfully manage all the moving parts of the conversation.

In the next chapter, we'll address the final moving part: the audience's role in helping you get the business of your presentation done.

Contents

Chapter 12
Facilitate Interactions

In this chapter . . .

- **This Is Not Just Q&A**
- **Defining Success**
- **Trust**
- **Staying Engaged**
- **Here's What Presenters Learned about Managing Interactions**
- **So What Does This Mean for You?**

This chapter focuses on how to manage interactions between you and your audience. These interactions can range from quick exchanges to long discussions involving everyone in your audience.

This Is Not Just Q&A

Once again, let's compare presentations to speeches. During a speech, interaction with the audience is intentionally limited. Typically, questions are allowed after the speech for a predetermined length of time. For example, a 20-minute speech might be followed by 10 minutes of questions. The speech itself isn't changed by the questions asked, and the questions are not a necessary part of the speech.

During your presentations, the audience's participation is necessary and inevitable. Sometimes you're interrupted by questions or comments. At other times, you ask the group questions or facilitate a discussion because you need input or feedback. No matter who initiates the exchange, the audience influences the pace of the presentation, its focus, and its outcomes.

The pace of Jennifer's presentation will be determined by how quickly her audience understands the information it's receiving. If there is confusion in the group, she will slow down or back up until everyone is ready to go on. Luis wants to be involved in a give-and-take with the VCs, and he knows that his ability to manage it will influence their decision. Michael's buyer may accept his proposal completely, or the two of them may reach a compromise deal. In each of these situations, the audience exerts its power and plays an active role in the conversation.

Just as it is throughout your presentation, the success of these interactions is measured on two levels: by how clear, concise, and accurate you are and by how well you facilitate the conversation taking place.

Is it okay to ask them to hold their questions?

From our perspective, asking people to hold their questions is appropriate in only two situations:

If you're running out of time and it's more important to get through the slides than it is to answer questions about them.

When the topic is one that needs to be taken in as a whole, and answering questions about its parts would detract from the big picture.

Otherwise, if it's merely your preference that questions be delayed, we always say no. It's better to be open to questions.

In some situations, the process goal is the only one you have control over. In every workshop, we've heard stories about audiences large and small, internal and external, that have been unwilling or unable to do what presenters are asking them to do. They refuse to buy, to learn, to commit, to embrace change. As with many other aspects of doing business, there are times when we have no control—or even much influence—over what other people do.

As frustrating as this is, it helps us focus on the right goals. We can turn away from the desire for perfect results and focus instead on creating the conditions required for a productive conversation.

Presenters succeed when they appropriately encourage and control the conversation taking place.

Defining Success

Let's define a successful interaction this way: presenters succeed when they appropriately encourage and control the conversation taking place. They create an environment in which the audience feels that information and ideas are freely exchanged, and the conversation is moving forward as efficiently as possible.

Let's look at these two goals for an interaction in more detail.

- **The audience feels that information and ideas are freely exchanged.** When someone comments or asks a question, you must appear open, interested, patient, and flexible. If you ask audience members to participate in discussions, the process should be relevant and necessary. The level of influence from individuals in the audience will vary, of course. Some people may have a lot to say and others nothing at all. What's important is not equal participation from everyone, but equal *opportunity* for participation.

- **The audience feels the conversation is moving forward as efficiently as possible.** Along with creating an open, safe environment for the conversation, you must control its progress. You need to manage time, stay focused on your goal, and prevent a single issue or person from dominating the conversation when they shouldn't.

Trust

These two goals compete with each other, of course, just like the other tensions involved in an Orderly Conversation. But, like Goldilocks, your audience members want the process to feel "just right." When it does, they will trust you to lead the conversation, and they will be more willing to do the work you're asking them to do.

Achieving these goals requires trust on your part as well. You have to believe the audience is acting in good faith and that the conversation will lead, eventually, to a good place. You also have to trust yourself to manage it. When I say that you have to trust yourself, I don't mean it as a you-can-do-it confidence builder. Believing in your ability to manage the conversation is a very practical thing. It helps you be a little fearless when interaction takes place. Without this level of trust in yourself you may do things that sabotage the conversation. Just as we've discussed in previous chapters, success requires staying engaged so that you can make the right decisions.

Staying Engaged

Think about the moment the first question or comment from your audience comes in. If you are like most people, you respond in one of two ways. Sometimes the interruption brings a sense of relief because it makes the process feel more conversational. At other times, the interruption feels like a threat—a threat to the plan you've created, to your knowledge or experience. This doesn't have to be a serious threat. It's just that you may feel the interruption comes at the wrong time or from someone you wish wouldn't interrupt at all. This is how Terry felt when his VP of Sales challenged him.

Both of these responses have to do with what you *feel* at the moment someone else begins to speak. Because this is an emotional reaction, it often leads to knee-jerk responses, very similar to those resulting from your Default Approach. If you're feeling threatened, you might be a little impatient or stubborn. If you welcome the interaction, as Michael typically does, you might spend too much time on it, losing sight of the framework of the presentation.

It's important for everyone, then, to be aware of and manage these immediate responses, just as you do throughout the presentation. Only now you have the additional responsibilities of understanding what someone else has said, fitting it into the presentation, and managing any emotion or attitude that may be attached to it.

Doing that requires you to remain engaged.

Remain Engaged

Eye Contact

We've discussed eye contact as the technique presenters use to initiate and sustain a conversational connection with audiences. When you're facilitating interactions, eye contact also helps you listen better and indicate where the focus of the group should go. When others are speaking, you should focus on them until they stop speaking. This has the same effect as directing people's focus to the screen by looking at it yourself. Your action will say, "Listen to what this person has to say. It's important."

Pausing

As you know, pausing will help you to stay in the moment and think on your feet. It's also a requirement for listening well and for appearing to listen well. So along with the role that pausing plays for you, it is also fundamental to the impression you make as a facilitator. In other words, the failure to pause—one of the most common problems presenters face during interactions—not only causes you to miss cues and misunderstand, it also discourages discussion because, without intending to, you appear impatient with or uninterested in what others have to say.

Let's break down this process into the four steps involved during an interaction between you and someone in your audience.

Step One: Pause to Listen

When a member of your audience starts to speak, your job is to pause and take in new information—not just the gist of what the audience member is saying, but all of the detail, nuance, and attitude that goes with it. In casual conversation, pausing and listening are fairly natural things to do. They're more difficult during your presentations, though, because they require letting someone else take control and believing that you'll be able to manage whatever happens.

As you listen, your eye contact should go to the person doing the talking. Again, in everyday conversation, we're all pretty good at that. We know our listening will be better if we stay focused on the other person. We also know that the other person will feel heard if we look like we're paying attention. Our parents' refrain of, "Look at me when I'm talking to you" has done its job.

If you don't fully understand what's been said, probe for clarification. If the question or comment is long, be sure to listen until the end without anticipating your response. Remember that the other people in the room are also observing the interaction you're having. So it's important to appear—and be—open and interested.

Step Two: Pause to Decide If Your Response Needs a Setup

Before you respond to what has been said, you have a couple of decisions to make. Do you need to say anything about the question—to contextualize or to clarify? If so, what do you need to say? These decisions are made based on both the audience's needs and yours.

- **For the audience's benefit.** When you're not sure if everyone heard the question, repeat what was said to bring everyone into the conversation. If the question is long or convoluted, the questioner may have lost the attention of the group. When that happens, it's a good idea to rephrase the question to keep everyone on track.

- **For your benefit.** Repeating or rephrasing a long, complex question also helps you shape your response. If you're asked a two-part question, for example, you might say, "Barbara is asking about a couple things. When will the project be complete, and what obstacles have we prepared for? Let's focus first on the obstacles."

Finally, when questions are emotional or hostile, simply naming the issue that has been brought up is preferable to repeating all of the details the question contained. Naming a difficult issue helps you control the tone in the room. "Lloyd brings up a lot of concerns about the customer service problems he's experienced over the last quarter." Naming the issue in this way validates Lloyd's complaints without naming all of them in detail.

Step Three: Deliver Your Response to Everyone

This is the most counterintuitive technique presenters need to master. Granted, sometimes you don't need to look at everyone in the audience when you respond—when the response is very short or of interest only to the person asking the question. But in situations where your response has relevance to the group, it's important to bring everyone into the conversation. When you do, you will shape your response for them and prevent the interaction from becoming an exclusive exchange between you and the questioner.

For example, suppose Dorothy fields this question from Joel, one of the regional managers in her audience.

Joel asks, "Dorothy, you mentioned that we are losing market share to low-end Sealed. And that's certainly true in my region. My buyers are all believers in low prices because it brings in more traffic, which results in more immediate sales. They don't really care whether their profit is coming from us or someone else."

Here are two ways Dorothy could manage this question.

- **Answer exclusively to Joel.** "Joel, that's exactly the point I'm trying to make. You need to help them see the long-term effects of this type of thinking. People who shop on price are not loyal customers. Next time they need something, they'll search for the cheapest, which may be somewhere else."

- **Answer generally to all.** "Joel makes a great point, and we all need to think about this—even those of you serving wealthier territories. Our buyers need to be reminded that low prices hurt both of us over the long term, because low-price shoppers are not loyal shoppers. Help your buyers see value in building loyal customers who buy based on the value of the product, not just low prices. If you can do that, we'll see our market share grow over the long term, just as we've seen in Dan's district after he used this approach with his team."

By choosing the second option, delivering her response to the group, Dorothy not only kept everyone in the conversation, but she also remembered to reinforce the importance of this issue to all of the salespeople. We understand that this technique flies in the face of proper etiquette. In every other situation at work and in life, people know that they should speak to the person who has spoken to them. Not doing so during a presentation feels odd. This is an important testament to the power of eye contact in conversation (remember

Grandma's admonition to look her in the eye and tell the truth). Nevertheless, staying engaged with the group will contribute to your success when answering questions.

Step Four: Pause to Decide Whether to Move on or Continue This Conversation

When you reach the end of your response, you have another decision to make. Would it be better to continue the interaction or move on with the presentation? If you want to continue, you have three options.

- If you want to make sure the question has been answered to the questioner's satisfaction, look at the questioner and ask for confirmation: "Did I answer your question?"
- If you think other people in the audience have similar concerns, ask the group if they have further questions about this topic.
- Would it be appropriate to bring in more questions about other topics? If so, you could say, "Before I go on, are there any other questions I can answer?"

If you want to move on, simply move back into your presentation. While this is often the appropriate thing to do, it requires real effort. Even if you've managed to deliver your answer to the group, the desire to check back in with the questioner, thereby continuing the interaction with that person, is strong.

The option you choose will determine how much control you exercise over the process. The decision to continue the interaction should always be made for the greater good. Even asking for confirmation, the first option listed in this step, gives control back to the individual and could lead to further conversation on a topic the group is not particularly interested in.

Let's look at how our participants manage the interactive process. They each found a way to balance the need for open dialog and efficiency.

What the Presenters Learned about Managing Interactions

It's the afternoon of the second day of the class. This is the final exercise in the workshop. During the exercise, the participants role-play for each other. While listening to one another's presentation, they do their best to jump into the shoes of each audience and ask questions based on the presenters' content. They try to be as realistic as possible as they comment on the presentation, ask questions, challenge the presenter, and, when appropriate, add humor or hostility to the interactions. As with all the other exercises, we made a video of each presentation. James went first.

Don't Interrupt: James

"How'd it go?" I asked James when we sat down to review his video.

"Fine," he replied, "but they said I didn't answer the question that was asked. They claim I interrupted Jennifer."

When we watched his video, we confirmed it: the group was right. As one of his potential buyers, Jennifer asked, "As you know, our products are delicate. What safeguards will you put in place to ensure everything arrives safely and free from electrostatic damage?"

He interrupted just as she said the word *arrives*. "We've always prided ourselves on our proprietary process for developing packaging to protect delicate products. We've worked with microchip makers, light bulb manufacturers, and bone china distributors, and everything in between. Don't worry. We'll take good care of your devices."

"What do you know? They were right. I did interrupt her. I get this question all the time. I gave her my standard answer. Dale talked about trying not to anticipate answers. I guess I'm guilty of that."

"Yes, and that could lose you the sale," I said. "Jennifer's question had two parts. One was about the safeguards you'll put in place to protect the customer's products from physical damage. The other was about static charge. You missed both parts of the question. And something else: you talked about irrelevant information. The light bulbs and bone china aren't very persuasive examples for this buyer."

He agreed, shaking his head in frustration. In every coaching session during the two days together, we came back to the same thing. James needs to be more aware of what's happening around him. During his presentations, that awareness starts with using his eye contact to engage in the conversation. If he's not seeing people—really seeing them—he'll never be perceived as a partner, and being a partner was one of the goals he set for himself. Had he been engaged when Jennifer asked her question, he would have heard the nuance of it. On a certain level, James understands this.

"Paying more attention to other people must be the new trick your wife was hoping you'd learn," I said.

After a moment of silence he said, "Be honest. Do I come off as arrogant? Kim slammed out of my office the other day mumbling something about how arrogant I am. I've heard it before, especially from my first wife."

I paused for a moment to gather *my* thoughts. "From what I've seen, James, yes. Sometimes you seem arrogant, or maybe impatient is a better term. Sorry to be so blunt. If you want to be a better communicator, you're going to have to be careful of that. You're really smart and passionate about what you do. Nothing wrong with that, but you don't need to be the strongest and smartest voice in every conversation. Let others have their say once in a while. And when they do speak? Look at them and listen. And try to reserve judgment."

Think on Your Feet: Michael

During Michael's presentation, Dorothy took on the role of Colleen, his buyer with the gymnast daughters. Early in his presentation, she said to him, "I see the shelves are empty again and there's no stock in back. How can I approve this promotion when there's nothing to put on the shelves?"

Michael asked me to pause the video. "This is the type of curve ball I mentioned yesterday morning," he said. "What am I supposed to say when I'm not even aware of the out-of-stock issue? It could be caused by a late delivery or a warehouse distribution thing, or even a recall. I can't make stuff up."

I said, "When you're engaged and focused on Colleen, you'll be able to think and decide what to say. Besides, the first thing that should happen is for you to acknowledge that Colleen is really frustrated. She knows you don't have control over every aspect of distribution. But right now, she wants to be heard and to have you take responsibility for the problem."

> **Stop talking already**
>
> **Most presenters worry a lot about the accuracy of their answers, leading to responses that are too long or complex. It's as if they need to prove their knowledge and keep going until they're fully satisfied with the response—even though everyone in the room got the point a long time ago.**

Work to Be Concise: Michael

As we got further into watching his video, Michael observed that he needed to be more concise. He explained, "Dorothy asked me whether I thought it was a good idea to spend the trade dollars right away and make a big splash. I should have said either yes or no. Instead, I did what Terry talked about yesterday morning. I said way too much. I see now that I need to rein it in. This sort of thing is why I have a hard time managing my time."

A better way to handle the trade dollar question would have been to pause and think, then provide the short answer. At that point, he should read his buyer's reaction and decide whether to go into more detail, or not. "Going into more detail," I reminded him, "should always be a thoughtful decision, not a knee-jerk reaction."

Answer to All: Luis

Luis was long-winded for a different reason. The question came from James. He asked, "It's nice that your sales are growing month over month. But what are you doing about the inevitable domestic competition? What about overseas patent and piracy issues that you must know are on their way?"

During his answer, Luis went on for much longer than necessary. Searching for the right words, he looked down at the floor. He shifted his weight several times and looked like he was making stuff up. What's more, he directed his entire answer in James's general direction but never made much of a connection with him. He finally finished with, "and as I've mentioned, the talent we will bring on board will have faced this sort of thing in previous companies. They will handle whatever comes their way."

James, as the VC, was out for blood. "And just how do you intend to keep this talent when the competition can and will offer them more cash and a bigger slice of the IPO pie?"

Looking to Dale, as if to surrender, Luis said, "My head's a mess, and that's pretty much how I suspect these things will go." He shook his head, "I need to be prepared for that and all the other questions I know they'll ask. Perfect role-play, by the way, James."

Dale kept the camera running and instructed James to ask the first question again. "This time, Luis, pause and breathe before you speak, then direct your answer to everyone in the room. James should become just another person—an important one, for sure—but just one more person in the room."

James asked the question again. This time Luis took a quick breath, nodded, and said directly to James, "You bring up two excellent questions, and many of the entrepreneurs you've seen today think a lot about these issues. First, we will need to stay on our toes and be vigilant." Luis set his eyes on people on the other side of the room and took a few steps toward them. "When funding comes through, we plan to invest in legal counsel overseas to address brand integrity issues as soon as they arise. Second," he directed this to James, "stateside, we will build a user community. . ." then he turned his focus toward others, "and invest in a dedicated team to host and monitor its activity. We believe this is the best way to build brand loyalty as well as a rich pipeline of user requests. We can't control the competition when it comes, but we can make 14 Ways the one and only go-to for our loyal customer base."

Watching the video, Luis said, "That's the guy I need to be up there. He was in control. And the pause wasn't as long as it felt."

I agreed. "That pause made you look controlled and thoughtful. The way you delivered the answer was very effective, and you remained respectful of James even though you engaged others in the answer. Also, I think you're more prepared than you think you are. You just need to think a little more about the questions you expect ahead of time, and then when they're asked, take a good pause before launching into the answer. That will give you the control you need to be clear and concise."

Deal with the Interruption, No Matter What: Sophia

Sophia said as she entered the video review room, "I'm feeling kinda sorry for the people I've trained over the last several years."

"What do you mean?" I asked.

"I finally understand why my boss, her name is Olive, wanted me to take this class. I've treated people like naughty schoolchildren. I even did it just now. I think Dale must have instructed Dorothy to ask a hostile question about something I hadn't covered yet. I literally threw up my hand as if to say stop. Then I told her to 'hang on' I'll get to that later.'"

We watched the video, and sure enough, it happened just as she said it did. Dale gave her a second chance, and here's how it went.

This time Sophia said, "The easy answer is yes. There will be a formal process for letting the Account Managers know about the opportunities. And you're right, it is another thing you'll have to do, but we've made it as user-friendly as possible. I'll cover that in a few minutes. For now, let's keep talking about why Member Service 2.0 is so important."

"That was so much better," she said. "I am going to have to show these videos to Olive. I know now what I need to do. I need to stay engaged, pause to think, keep my focus on them, and go where they want to go. I mean, just there, when I had a chance to redeem myself, I was so much more effective. Dale talked earlier about being respectful and in return, earning their trust. I get that now."

"I'm glad," I said, "I think I would enjoy learning from Sophia 2.0."

Listen—and Appear to Listen, Too: Elaine

During Elaine's presentation, Dale assigned Michael to be a concerned citizen. Michael interrupted Elaine and asked a roundabout question regarding the timing of construction around St. Patrick's Day. Elaine couldn't remember the exact date, so while Michael rambled on, she rifled through her notes. All Elaine was trying to do was keep things moving at a good pace. Watching her video, she said, "They were right, I looked impatient with him."

As Dale mentioned earlier, you control the focus of the room. Not only did Elaine look impatient, she also sent mixed signals to the rest of the audience. Where were they to look? It's true they *may* have stayed attentive to Michael. The likelihood of that would have been greater had Elaine kept all of her attention on Michael and waited for him to finish. All she'd need to do after he had finished speaking is say something like, "I can't remember the exact date, but if you give me just a moment to look… ah, yes. Here it is…"

Avoid Rating Questions and Checking Back In: Dorothy

Terry asked Dorothy a question about the fire issue and whether a health hazard was associated with the chemicals they use in their asphalt shingles. Dorothy said, "That's a great question. It's my understanding, based on the conversation I had with Paul in R&D, that it's a very low risk, but it should not be dismissed as benign. Did that answer your question?"

"Was it really a great question?" I asked.

"No. It wasn't," she said.

"Then why did you say it was?"

"Habit. Probably should put that in check, huh?"

"Probably," I replied. "It's not that rating a question is a horrible thing to do. But if you do it all the time, it ultimately means nothing. Also, why did you ask him if your response had answered his question?"

"Habit. I'll put that in check too."

"Well…sort of. I'm not saying you should never check back in with a questioner," I said. "We've talked a lot about how staying engaged helps you think on your feet. This is an example of that. Checking back in should be a decision, not a habit."

Dealing with Virtual Attendees Who Are Dialing Into a Live Presentation

If you are like Dorothy and have to manage virtual and in-person attendees in the same presentation, remember that you have responsibility to both audience groups. Follow the recommendations for using directional language and:

- **Ask virtual attendees to put their phones on mute, and encourage them to use the chat feature if they have questions or comments.**
- **Assign someone else to monitor chat and be the spokesperson for the virtual attendees.**
- **Check in with the virtual attendees throughout by asking if they have anything they'd like to add to the conversation.**

Questions Are Not Threats: Dorothy

"One last thing," I said to Dorothy, "before you go. Early yesterday, you asked a question about how to deal when people ask you all sorts of questions and pull you in several directions at once. I got the sense that you thought of their questions as threats to your knowledge."

"That's true, I did. But I see now that they were asking those questions because I was confusing them and not managing the conversation very well. Now that I know how to organize the information better, and I know how to manage the group dynamics, I don't think that will be an issue any more."

"That's great," I said.

Name the Issue: Jennifer

Jennifer barely got started before having to deal with interactions from her audience. As part of her introduction, she said, "and the reason we're doing this is so that we can all get reimbursed more quickly."

James said, "We'd better. Last year after my trip to the annual conference in Seattle, it took 13 weeks for my reimbursement check to arrive. Totally unacceptable."

Elaine piled on with, "Same thing here after my conference in D.C. That trip was a week long, and the meals alone added up to over a thousand dollars. There were so many receipts to deal with, *and* I had to subtract liquor expenses—it took me several tries to get it all submitted and approved."

"I know, it's just crazy. Why we even have to cover our own expenses up front is ridiculous," harrumphed Luis.

Jennifer looked to Dale and called a timeout. "This is exactly what is going to happen, but I don't know what to do. I remember you said that when something like this happens, we should do something...what was it? I'm in the funhouse and can't think straight."

"Name the issue," said Dale from behind the camera.

"Right," she said, continuing, "I know. I hear you. The old process was labor intensive and slow. We have all experienced similar things. That's why we've put this new process in place. So, let's not wait one minute longer." She advanced the slide. "Here's the three-step process."

Use a Negative Question to Reinforce Your Point: Terry

Terry asked the group to be as rough on him as they could. He said that he'll face really tough questions, and he wants to be prepared. "No softballs, okay?"

They let him get through half of his presentation before they started. He brought up the slide about next year's budget. He said, "As you can see, the budget I'm asking for is nearly double what was projected..."

The group interrupted him with statements like these:

"What?"

"Sure, IT always asks for (and gets) more than their fair share of the budget."

"The way you managed this year's budget, what makes you think we'd trust you with one dime more?"

On the video, it was hard to know who said what.

Here's how Terry handled it. First he paused to think. He walked over to the laptop, hit the letter *B* on the keyboard, and walked to the center of the room. Then he said, "You're all concerned about this budget. I don't blame you. When I saw the preliminary numbers, I questioned them too. But if you'll allow me to dig a little deeper in the next few slides, you'll see that the infrastructure investment that I'm proposing worldwide will save money in several ways.

"First, at least three people at each location need to go through intense training to administer the current system. Thanks to the workload for those people, the turnover is extremely high, and new people need to be trained all the time. That won't be an issue anymore, since the new system doesn't require much training. And those three people can be moved over to help their colleagues who, as we know, are overworked as it is. That's a win-win.

"Second, we're currently outsourcing data backup. That's a security risk that will be completely eliminated once we transition to the new system. That's a win-win too. We stop paying for a third party, and our data is more secure.

"Third, the server rooms will run cooler, so there will be energy savings there.

"And finally, I have no idea how to calculate this, but the systems will run faster across the entire enterprise, and who wouldn't like that?"

Terry paused again to see if anyone had anything else to add. They didn't, so he brought his slides back up on the screen and said, "So, yes, these numbers are high. Let's look at them in more detail..."

"And let's end there," said Dale. "Nice job, Terry."

When Terry and I reviewed his video, he seemed extremely pleased. "You're smiling as you watch this," I observed.

"That guy has executive presence," he said.

"Yes, he does."

What's up with the B key?

Sometimes the slide on the screen becomes a distraction to the conversation taking place. When that happens (and assuming your slideware has this feature), you can simply hit the B key to make the screen go black.

Doing this communicates that the slide content is no longer the focus of the conversation. Something else is. Then, when it's time to return to the slide, all you need to do is hit any key on the keyboard or remote and the slide will come back on the screen.

So What Does This Mean for You?

In everyday, low-stakes conversations, you probably manage the give-and-take of group interaction well. But during business presentations, the stakes are higher—there's a goal that needs to be met as efficiently as possible. This is why it's so important to create an environment in which a fruitful conversation can take place.

If you establish trust with your audience, avoid knee-jerk reactions, and make decisions on the fly, you should be able to manage the process with ease. But things aren't that easy when you're nervous or when listeners pull you in different directions. It's even more difficult when things get emotional. Therefore, remember to pause and breathe so that you can make thoughtful decisions. The presentation may not go as planned, but that's okay. What's important is maintaining the quality of the conversation and getting business done.

We still need to tie up a few loose ends for the class participants. We'll do that in the final chapter.

Contents

Chapter 13
Wrap Up

In this chapter . . .
- **Charting the Wrap Up Discussion**
- **Getting Business Done**

Greg:

At the end of each workshop, when the camera is off and the last video has been reviewed, I stand next to the flipchart at the front of the room. At the top of the chart I have written "Major discoveries and areas to work on."

I go around the room filling in the chart for each person. As we've said, improvement is achieved by the ripple effect of a few simple changes in approach, attitude, or habit. At this point in a workshop, everyone knows what those changes are.

Improvement is achieved by the ripple effect of a few simple changes in approach, attitude, or habit.

Charting the Wrap Up Discussion

"Terry, you kicked things off yesterday morning, so let's start with you again."

Terry: A Writer

Terry came into the workshop to learn the rules of presenting. He got the direction he needed, but not the one-size-fits-all rules he was looking for. His focus now is on engaging his listeners. He discovered that once he does that, other issues, such as what to do with his hands, will take care of themselves.

He asked early on about the best way to prepare and "get started." He has the tools for that now, too. He also understands how to put his love for detail in check. Because Terry is a Writer, though, doing that will probably never feel comfortable. Nonetheless, he knows what he needs to do to reach his goals.

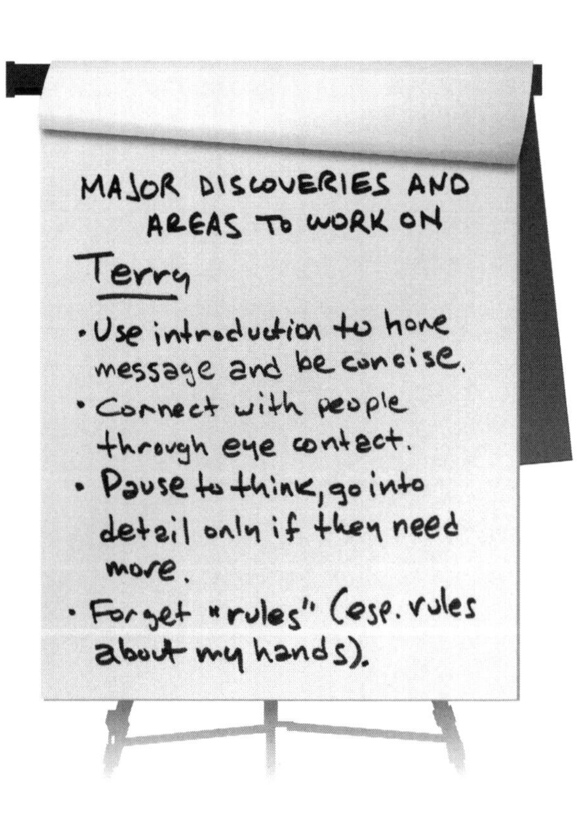

How he'd like to be perceived

- Executive presence
- Clear
- Concise
- In control

Dorothy: An Improviser

Dorothy delivers detailed information to people who have to turn it around and deliver it to buyers. Her assumption had always been that simply providing the information was enough. She learned that her focus needs to shift to making sure what she says is understood and useful. To do so required rethinking how she prepares and presents her information. Luckily, she became comfortable with the framing strategy early on, and everything else fell into place. She said to me, "I thought I had to do something monumental to be more interesting. Instead, all I need to do is help them understand and make the information practical for them. That's what they'll find interesting." It's also what will make her appear more strategic.

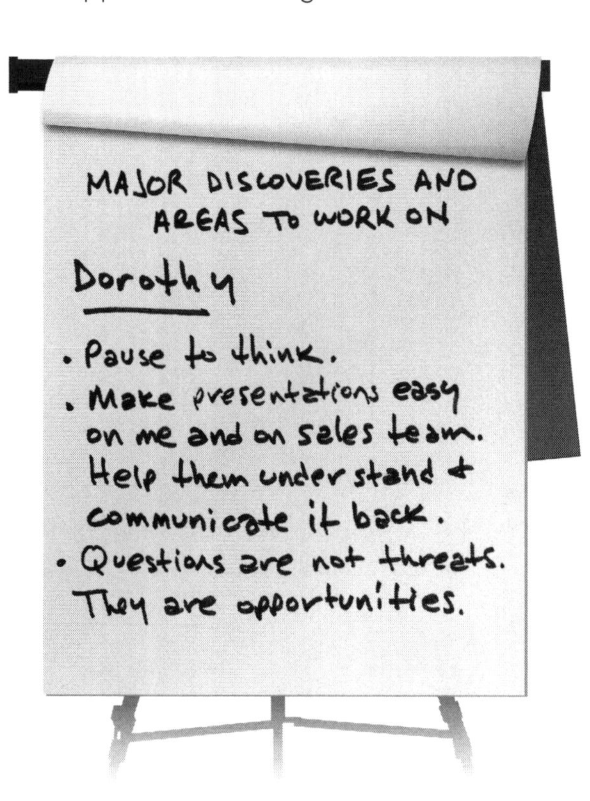

How she'd like to be perceived

- Helpful
- Strategic
- Knowledgeable

Michael: An Improviser

Michael came into the workshop with a good set of skills, but he needed to manage his one-on-one sales situations better.

Two things will help him close the sale more efficiently: clarifying what he wants his buyer to do, and managing his time. These two things don't come naturally to most Improvisers, but he learned how to do both. Pausing will help Michael think on his feet and handle the curve balls. When he pauses, he's able to manage the twists and turns of the conversation, even when things get emotional. Michael's confidence also got a boost when he saw on video that already he appears honest, on their side, helpful, and trustworthy.

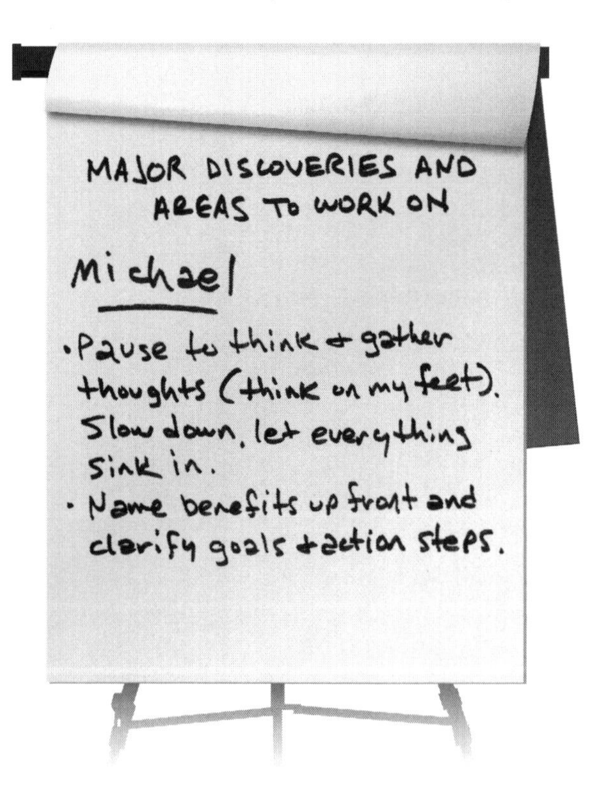

How he'd like to be perceived

- Honest
- On their side
- Helpful
- Trustworthy
- Not a used-car salesman

Jennifer: A Writer

While there is no cure for anxiety, Jennifer learned how to manage her nerves. She realizes now that rehearsal and scripting are not helpful and that preparing to be flexible is. This is a major shift in her thinking. As she saw on video, she is clear and professional when she lets go of perfection, pauses to think, and focuses on her audience.

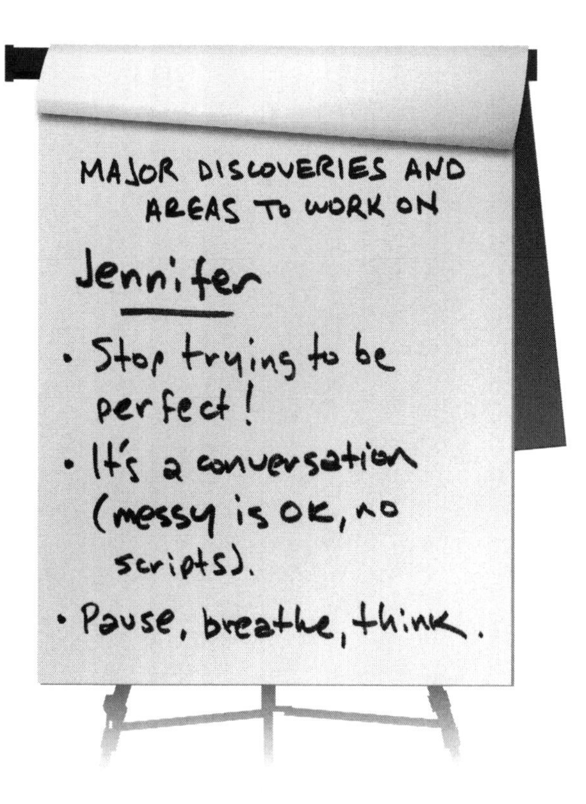

How she'd like to be perceived

- Professional
- Clear
- Concise
- Know my stuff

James: An Improviser

James wanted "new tricks." What he got was an objective look at himself. The main issue for him was his lack of self-awareness. He learned that if he wants to be perceived as a partner and a team player, he needs to turn his focus outward and read people better.

At the end of the workshop, while others were gathering their belongings, James walked up to me, shook my hand and said, "I really didn't want to come to this workshop, but I'm glad I did. I finally understand how I come across to the others. When I get back to the office, I'm going to ask my employees to call me on my arrogance. I think that's the only way I'll become more aware of it. Thanks."

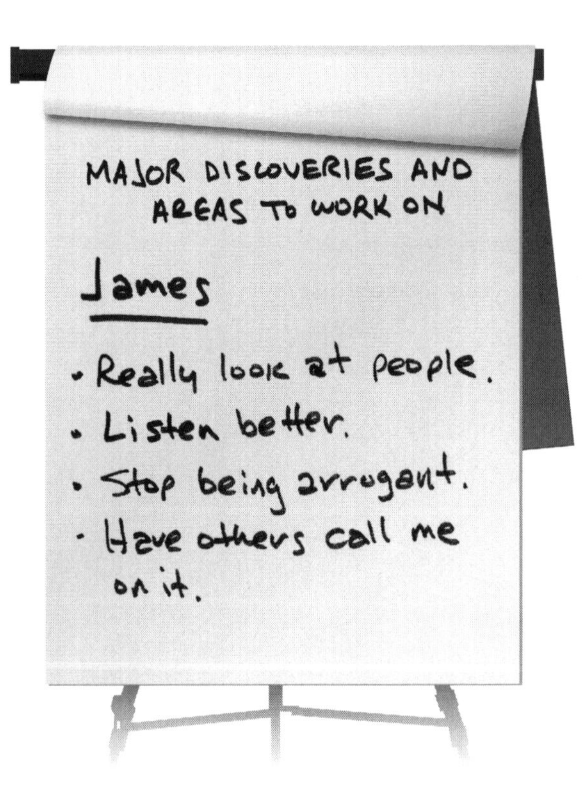

How he'd like to be perceived

- Partner
- Team player
- Solid
- Good reputation

Sophia: A Writer

Like others, Sophia entered the class with some troublesome rules (memorizing), gimmicks (icebreakers), and assumptions (desire to entertain). She learned that all of these things were actually having the opposite effect from what she intended. She also came to realize that engaging people in a genuine conversation should be her first priority.

She did really well, so I'm sure Sophia will keep her job.

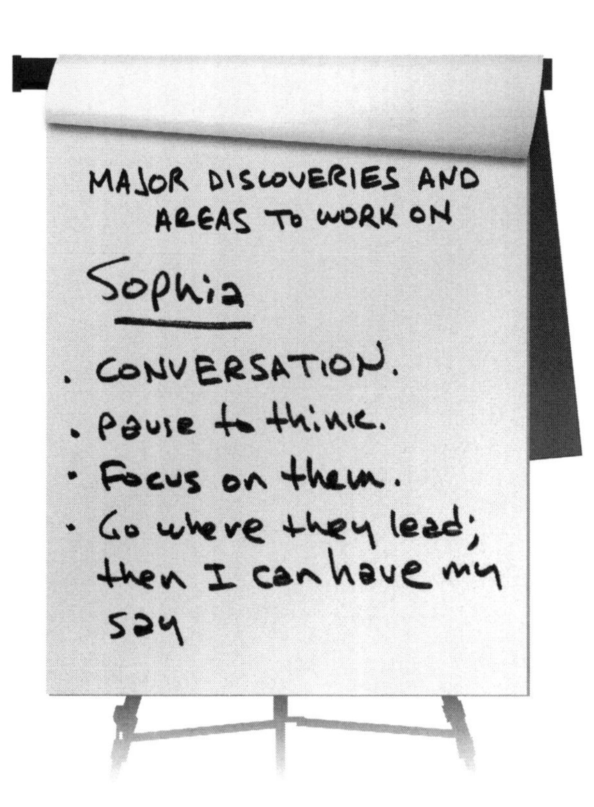

How she'd like to be perceived

- Entertaining
- Fun
- Genuine
- Clear
- Professional

Luis: An Improviser

Luis is struggling to adjust to his new role as a business leader. However, he made great progress in the workshop. He understands his Default as an Improviser, and he has a fresh set of tools to build the structure he and his listeners need. He may look young for his age, but when he watched himself taking questions and comments from his audience, he saw a mature businessperson. He was a focused, capable professional. That alone will boost his confidence when he and his team face the VCs.

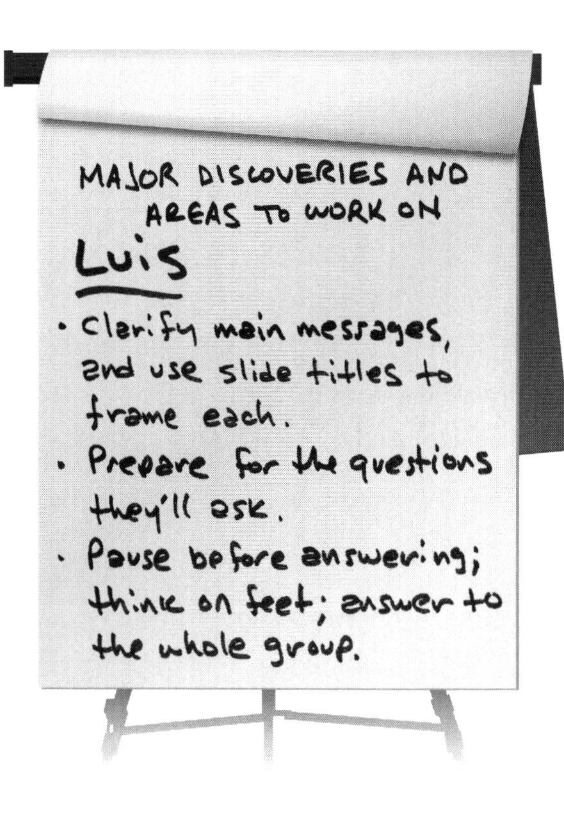

How he'd like to be perceived

- Professional
- Trustworthy
- Mature
- Capable

Elaine: A Writer

Initially, Elaine wanted to learn techniques for detaching herself emotionally from her presentations. She assumed this would keep her from "turning to mush" when emotions run high. What she learned was something else: that empathy goes a long way. By acknowledging her audience's very real concerns, she'll be in a better position to initiate a fruitful conversation with them.

At one point during our coaching session, Elaine added empathetic to her list of goals. I was glad she did.

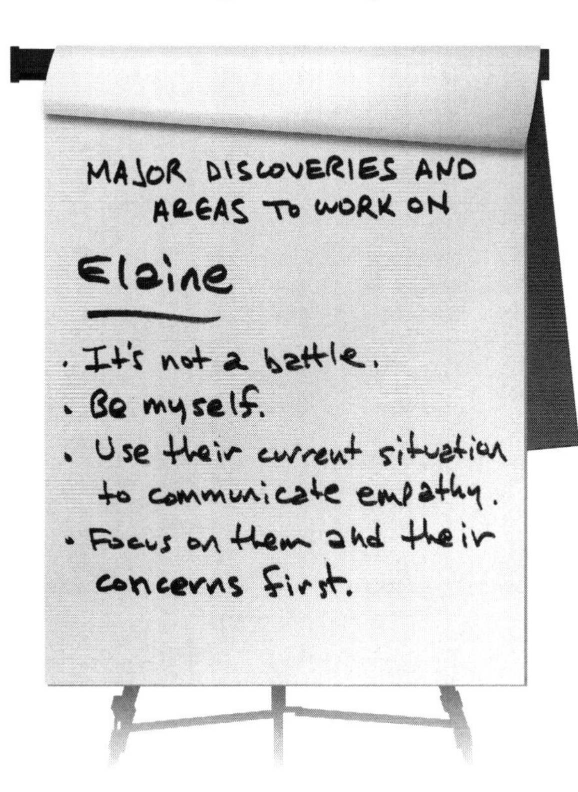

How she'd like to be perceived

- In control
- Strong

Midway through the workshop, she added

- Empathetic

Getting Business Done

At the end of every workshop, we restate the goals we set out to reach when the class began. We want everyone to walk away feeling more confident, more comfortable, and in control of their presentations. As we've seen with Jennifer, Michael, Sophia, Terry, Elaine, Luis, Dorothy, and James, achieving those goals always means something different for everyone.

For you, our reader, we said at the outset that this book was written to help you get business done, to make your business presentation responsibilities no more challenging than any other part of your job. We hope we've done that by redefining the process in a way that makes sense to you and following the effect of that redefinition through each step of the process.

More than anything else, we hope *The Orderly Conversation*® has brought a sigh of relief, a spark of recognition, and renewed faith in your ability to succeed.

Acknowledgements

We are grateful for the support of so many people during the process of writing this book.

First, we would not have made it to the finish line without the guidance of John Capecci and support of Tim Cage at Granville Circle Press. The fact that John and Tim brought Brad Norr and Chris Thillen into the project makes their contribution even greater.

Thank you to all the people who are or have been part of the Turpin Communication team since 1992. To our first readers, Mary Clare Healy, Milena Palandech, Dana Peters, Blaine Rada, and Sarah Stocker, thanks for your perspective and smart questions. We also want to thank Lora Alejandro, Laura Jane Bailey, Jeanne Cotter, Janice Funk, Conor Healy, Seth Kanoff, Adam Kirby, Anne Linehan, and Karen Ross.

Barbara Egel, thank you for an inspiring substantive edit. To Kay Holley, Mary Ann Murphy, Dan Myers, Barbara Schwarzentraub, and Lloyd Schwarzentraub, thanks for being excellent resources.

To our friends at the Chicagoland Chapter of the Association for Talent Development (formerly the Chicagoland Chapter of ASTD), thanks for your support.

Finally, we thank our friend, Renee Myers. Although she did not live long enough to see it in print, Renee's support for this book will always be remembered. When Renee asked, "How's that book coming, Dale?" (as she often did over the span of several years) it was always with deep interest and encouragement.

Turpin Communication is a presentation and facilitation skills training company based in Chicago, IL. We work with presenters, facilitators, and trainers in all industries and at all levels of experience.

Everything we do is designed to help people get business done. While a particular workshop or coaching engagement may focus on a very specific business goal—closing a deal, making a decision, learning something new, or gaining alignment—our overall goal is to help presenters be more comfortable, effective, and confident in the work they do.

The authors are available for workshops, key note addresses and to speak at conferences and corporate meetings.

For information, contact

engage@theorderlyconversation.com

Visit our websites at

www.TurpinCommunication.com or

www.TheOrderlyConversation.com

linkedin.com/company/turpin-communication

@TurpinComm

facebook.com/TurpinCommunication

Index

Granville Circle
PRESS
Communicating good ideas.